Secrets from the Inside:

How to Buy a New Car Below Dealer Cost

Introducing the

No-Enemies Buying Method

By Greg Meakin

Published by U.S. Publishing

Copyright © 1991 by U.S. Publishing, a division of U.S. Marketing Network, Inc.

ISBN: 0-9631181-0-2

First Edition
First Printing, 1991

Editorial Consultant---R.D.R. Hoffmann
Editor---Walker Roberts
Photography---Vance Photography
Administrative Assistant---Roberta Johnson
Printer---Rose Printing Co., Inc.,
Creative Consultant---Roberts & Hice Inc.
Typesetter: Tampa Type

For information contact:
U.S. Publishing
509-A N. Tamiami Trail
Venice, FL 34292

Dedication

Someone once said if you want a long lasting, happy marriage, marry your best friend. This book is lovingly dedicated to my best friend, my wonderful wife, my inspiration, my faithful source of guidance--Deborah.

I also wish to celebrate the 60th wedding anniversary of my grandparents, Leslie and Dorothy Sutcliffe of Montreal. A diamond anniversary is truly a remarkable achievement. Here's to many more, Nana and Papa.

Table of Contents

Acknowledgements

I wish to deeply thank my friend, Richard Hoffmann, who is a freelance writer in Clearwater, Florida. Richard's editorial contribution made this book possible.

I also would like to thank Walker Roberts, with Roberts Communications & Marketing, Inc., in Tampa, Florida. As the former editor of several magazines, including Florida Trend, Walker brought years of experience to bear in the final production of *Secrets from the Inside*.

Also, my heartfelt appreciation is extended to Roberta Johnson, my wonderful secretary. She spent weeks typing the original, hand written manuscript of this book.

Nor can I fail to recognize here the contribution of Carolyn Permentier, an advertising professional, who helped shape the basic look of the cover of this book.

Foreword

In the mid-'60s, when I was a new car salesman in Detroit, we referred to the customers as "mooches." Unfortunately, things haven't changed much since then.

Buying a new vehicle today is not much different than it was for your father, or grandfather for that matter. Auto dealerships, and their salespeople in particular, are still playing the old game of "beat the mooches."

After leaving the car business for a career on Wall Street, I always dealt with owners or their managers directly, bypassing my many salesman "friends" when buying a new vehicle. Why did I employ this method? Simply because it was the smart thing to do, as you'll see in this book.

Greg Meakin "opens the kimono" of the car business with his new book, *Secrets from the Inside,* and in doing so surely reduces the number of "mooches" lining up to buy new cars and trucks in the U.S.

Over the last several years, my firm, University Consultants Inc., has been studying the U.S. auto dealership industry. Early indications of positive change are emerging from this dinosaur-like industry, like greater emphasis on customer satisfaction. But the sales process is still antiquated, and in my opinion it's counter productive, yet the industry persists in doing business in a manner that can only be called adversarial.

Until the industry itself realizes that its sales practices create apprehension and ill-will among customers, not to mention personnel headaches and unnecessary expense for dealerships, cars and trucks will be sold the same old way. That doesn't mean that you have to become a victim, however. Arm yourself with *Secrets from the Inside*, use Greg Meakin's "no-enemies" approach to buying your next vehicle, and keep you hard-earned dollars where they belong--in **your** pocket.

L. Joseph Schmoke

President

University Consultants, Inc.

Note: L. Joseph Schmoke is author of *Vital Business Secrets,* published by Dow Jones-Irwin, 1989.

Preface

It was in 1989 in Seattle, during one of those all-too-often 14-hour shifts as a sales manager in an automobile dealership, that I was confronted with an occurrence that caused me to promise myself that "some day" I would speak out to American consumers and car dealers alike.

A combative type of car buyer was attempting to find the best deal possible on a Ford Escort. When I say combative, I mean a an individual who openly refuses to believe that any person in business today, much less a "car person," can be trusted.

After this customer and my salesman haggled more than two hours, I decided to intervene.

Sitting down with the customer, I said, "Mr. Smith, since you seem to be here to buy an Escort at the best possible price, I will sell you the Escort of your choice for dealer invoice."

I showed the customer the actual invoice on the chosen car. He looked at me suspiciously, and said wryly: "That's a good deal, but how do I know that this is the actual invoice, that you didn't doctor it?"

I was stunned. This man felt that I would create a phony invoice to gain a couple of hundred dollars in markup, with all the future exposure that illegal act would invite. I was amazed and insulted, and asked that he leave the dealership.

In time, I came to understand that this person had been taught, and had embraced, mistrust as a rule he followed whenever he did business--especially buying cars. The paradox was that he wanted to be dealt with honestly. When I did that, he refused to believe it.

Many of the arguments I present in this book were prompted by my experience with Mr. Smith. I came to recognize that most people dread the car buying process because they have no idea how to correctly go about it. When I say "correctly," I mean paying as close to dealer invoice as possible, and doing so without the notorious combat and hassle associated with new car purchasing.

I will, indeed, introduce information tools available to you as a car shopper, and present a simplified method to apply that information that will allow you pay the lowest possible price.

At the same time, it is my theory that the No-Enemies "win-win" attitude and philosophy can be applied in many areas of people's lives. So, when you read through this simple buying method, I invite you to also read between the lines.

Greg Meakin

CHAPTER I

NO-ENEMIES

Every car buyer--most of the U.S. population with a driver's license--could tell an animated story about being financially victimized by a car dealer. But few of these stories are told since people do not like to admit to being taken.

Ask anyone how well they did on the price of the new car they just bought, and most will say with a confidential wink and knowing nod that they did "real good," or "fine," or "just great" or something equally vague, despite the facts.

Pressed, some may say that their deal was well below "sticker"--that sheet of paper the dealer glues to one of the side windows of the car, listing its features and total price--which most people know is a heavily marked-up retail price packed with profit for the dealer.

But, even if they paid $1,000 or even $2,000 below the sticker price, some car buyers realize, or at least suspect, that they still spent more than they had to for the car--no matter what "extra" feature was "thrown in" by the dealer.

An even more common reason that those tales of car-buying woes go unheard is that most people don't know they've been taken. The psychology and practice of car salesmanship is such that, even if buyers are lead down the garden path only to wind up in the briar patch, they most often believe they are in a bed of roses. They suppress any unhappiness or negative perceptions simply because they want the deal to be wonderful.

Their downfall then can be accomplished with such finesse that buyers will often remain oblivious to the manipulations of the sales person, and become willing participants in their own fleecing.

Whose fault is this state of affairs, where buyer is pitted against seller? Is it the car dealer's?

It is true that the retail car business has become synonymous with devious selling practices, using everything from high-pressure sales tactics to misleading advertising claims. As in any human endeavor, there are bound to be a number of blatantly dishonest money grabbers or outright con artists among car dealers, just as there are sure to be poor businessmen and lousy administrators.

Others simply take what the traffic will bear. This doesn't make them bad, but rather a lot like many people in the world, who take as much as they can get away with as long as they are allowed to.

Most car dealerships are like any other American business. Their goal and purpose is to make a profit, and thus be financially able to continue to offer products and services to their customers. They can defend their selling practices, certainly to their own satisfaction, with logical and compelling reasons.

What of the argument, then, that car buyers' unhappiness is their own fault? Who, after all, allows car dealers to get away with these things?

Most of the car-buying public still walks into a dealership with little knowledge of what they're about to do. Many show up on the showroom floor with such hazy and indefinite requirements that they are asking to be sold a car instead of wanting to buy a car.

Too many car buyers allow themselves to be at the mercy of sales representatives whose entire professional life is devoted to understanding customers in order to sell four-wheeled vehicles at the highest possible profit to the dealership and themselves.

A couple of decades ago, consumer groups decided that the blame lies squarely with the car industry, from the manufacturer on down. Those consumer advocates have done an excellent job of making buyers aware of problems with the car industry's products and services, with dealer fraud and misrepresentation, and with consumers' rights.

Unfortunately, they have also evolved car-buying systems that assume that the car-buying process would forever be a contentious struggle between customer and retailer. Such buying methods promote an aggressive and adversarial negotiating stance, creating opinionated, abrasive consumers whose idea of buying a car means browbeating sales people into submission.

All that those systems have accomplished is to entrench the "us vs. them" mentality toward car buying, with each side determined to win the battle. Those systems and attitudes have only created enmity between car buyers and car dealers.

This fault-finding between consumers and retailers is hardly an optimum situation. Unless one really wants to fight on some imaginary field of consumer combat to get even with car dealers and sales people for past improprieties, what good is walking into a dealership with a chip on your shoulder?

All most folks want to do is buy a car, and not feel cheated in the process.

Fortunately, today's economic pressures have forced the car industry in general and dealers in particular to pay more attention to quality, value, and service if they want to continue doing business. The chances of finding a "good" dealer are greater than ever before.

The ever-present threat of consumer action helps sustain the renewal of emphasis on craftsmanship in manufacture, of fairness in sales practices, and of attention to customer needs that is becoming more and more evident in today's car industry.

As such, now is the time to stop fighting, and to buy your next new car at a drastically reduced wholesale price that could be thousands of dollars below dealer cost, if one or more factory rebates apply. That's right, thousands of dollars below dealer cost, minus the combat!

This book will tell you how. *Secrets from the Inside* details the No-Enemies Buying Method , a simple, seven-step process which removes all the aggression and antagonism that car buyers and dealers have been visiting on one another.

It uncovers some high technology new-car buying information sources that become the key to success in negotiations. It offers precise instructions on how to use that information, as well as when and where to take each step.

It defines who to go to and who to stay away from. It explains specifically how to negotiate a new-car purchase, save a bundle of money, and become a happy, satisfied and confident car buyer who won't need to blame anyone about anything.

It shows you exactly what to do before, during and after your purchase to both get the car you want at a great price and the respect and loyalty of any car dealer with whom you choose to do business. The method allows car buyers to assert themselves by taking control of their own car-buying destiny, assisted by knowledge of the car industry.

Here's a preview to give you a look at the simple logic of the method. Each step will be explained in detail in later chapters. (There is an expanded outline of the method in Chapter X that can be used as a checklist.)

THE NO-ENEMIES BUYING METHOD

STEP 1: **GATHERING INFORMATION**

STEP 2: **EVALUATING A TRADE-IN**

STEP 3: **ARRANGING FINANCING**

STEP 4: **SEARCHING FOR DEALERS**

STEP 5: **DRIVING AND DEALING**

STEP 6: **CLOSING THE DEAL**

STEP 7: **TAKING DELIVERY & FOLLOWING UP**

The No-Enemies Buying Method is just that--a method. This book presents a practical framework for car buying. The method details and encourages--in fact, requires--the input and assistance of other consumer and automotive publications, as will be specifically related later on.

Some information services, such as those that give the factory-to-dealer cost of new cars, are very valuable in terms of their step-saving convenience.

The No-Enemies Buying Method, it should be understood, may require that consumers do battle, but not with car dealers or sales people. The real battle will be against the only true enemy which can defeat car buyers: Themselves!

Some car buyers are their own worst enemies. They can be taken advantage of because they lack three very important things: knowledge, confidence, and a responsible plan of action.

The No-Enemies Buying Method supplies all three.

CHAPTER II

THE NEW-CAR
DEALER

The first requirement for success with the No-Enemies Buying Method must be an understanding of the new-car dealership organization. That understanding begins with specific knowledge of how dealerships are structured and who populates them.

1. THE PEOPLE

Most people know that car dealerships have two faces-- sales and service--and that there are sales people and managers that deal with the public.

Consumers are also likely to be aware that sales people get paid through a commission structure, which might be a percentage of the price of the car, or the profit.

That dealership system is designed for the highest possible profit, and allows the dealer to control the car-buying process. Control is gained through the individuals with whom a customer actually deals when buying a new car.

These include a sales person, a new-car sales manager, a used-car sales manager, a service manager, a finance and insurance manager, and a general manager.

Although the No-Enemies Buying Method does not require negotiations with anyone but the sales manager, the business inter-relationships, operational responsibilities and financial motives of the car dealership team are important to know because they explain the dealership system.

Sales people are the best place to begin this investigation.

SALES PEOPLE

Generally there are only two types of automotive sales people: Good ones and bad ones. Whatever their description, they are typically paid by commission, usually between 18 and 25 percent of the gross profit of any car that they sell.

The gross profit is the difference between what the dealer initially pays the factory for the car and the price the customer winds up paying. A dealer's gross profit on a car sale generally ranges from 10% to 15%.

The net profit (the gross profit minus the dealer's cost of doing business) is a different story: industry-wide estimates put the average net profit for a dealership below 3%.

A car dealership's cost of doing business includes everything from pencils to people--and, as can be expected in today's economic climate, these things are not getting any cheaper. This puts pressure on dealerships to sustain a high gross profit, which translates to the car buyer as inflated selling prices.

The selling price usually includes what is known as "dealer pack", a car industry term that describes a dealership's charge to every deal intended to partially off-set that high cost of doing business. This is normally around 1% of the selling price or slightly higher, and is subtracted from the selling price before the sales person's commission is figured.

When the selling price is at or near dealer invoice, a min-imum or "flat" commission, usually between $75 and $150, is paid to sales people in lieu of their full commission rate.

Sales people also receive "spiffs" or bonuses for individ-ual sales performances. These bonuses can be awarded by either the dealership or the factory, with factory-sponsored programs amounting to hundreds or even thousands of dol-lars a month.

While remuneration issues help us understand the forces on the sales force, these factors will not be the concern of the customer using the No-Enemies Buying Method. So, let's consider what makes sales people good or bad.

The bad ones are simply poorly trained, or have personal-ities that are not attuned to customer wants or needs. Some well-trained bad sales people are fast-talking wolves who rudely accost customers, while others are little lambs who jump if the customer says "boo."

Either type seems to be congenitally deaf to any proposal that deviates from the dealership system. Mention the words "invoice" or "dealer cost"--which, as readers will learn later on, are key to the No-Enemies Buying Method--and the wolves and the lambs will appear close to a nervous breakdown.

When customers are made to feel comfortable, when they have a sense that their needs and wants are understood and that they are being paid attention to, it is certain that the sales person they are dealing with is a good one.

Good sales people are adaptable creatures, willing to wear many role-playing hats. They ask probing questions about your wants and needs; questions that sometimes have an agenda behind them, and sometimes are just asked out of curiosity.

Good sales people act as if they are devoted agents for the customer when it comes down to pricing and options on a new car. They have the ability to make the customer believe that they can give the customer the best possible deal on exactly what they want.

So, consumers should seek out good sales people to buy cars from, and stay away from the bad ones, right? Wrong!

The idea is not to initiate or close a deal with a new-car sales person of any description, period! The reason is simple: Good or bad, they all are controlled by the dealership selling system.

If you have a friend at a dealership, and you send your son or daughter to see them about a new car, they will probably do the best that they can. But the best that most can do is sell within the parameters laid down by the sales manager and the dealership system.

Ultimately, sales people within that system are interested in selling cars to gain the highest possible profit for the dealership and the highest possible commission for themselves.

The absolutely best deal for the customer--such as can be attained through the No-Enemies Buying Method--is usually the worst possible deal for the sales person.

SALES MANAGERS

There are usually two types of sales managers in a dealership, one responsible for used-car sales and the other for new-car sales. Larger stores often have corresponding truck managers and fleet managers.

They are all, along with the finance and insurance manager, the service manager and other specialists, part of the dealerships middle-management layer.

The used-car sales manager is responsible for directing the "previously owned" car sales of dealerships. Later on you will find out how important this area is in dollar terms to the consumer. In a new-car purchase, consumers normally will not deal with the used-car manager directly, but rather indirectly; the "trade-in allowance" toward the purchase price of a new car is governed by the appraisal of the used-car department.

New-car sales managers are the individuals that consumers should be dealing with directly with the No-Enemies Buying Method. Fleet managers are also appropriate for the consumer to deal with. Fleet managers tend to have corporations as clients, and sell at wholesale prices.

These managers also have the responsibility and authority to make decisions that will affect the profit structure of a customer's car deal.

Operationally, sales managers are specifically in charge of organizing, directing and motivating new-car sales people; of overseeing lot attendants and other dealer support staff; of new-car advertising, as well as liaison with upper management and dealing with factory orders. They take a broad view of sales in general, and are not tied as tightly to the profit on individual car sales as sales people are.

As a rule, their income is based on the overall performance of the sales department. Although pay plans for sales managers vary widely, they most often involve some percentage of the gross profit of the sales department and possibly others, such as the finance and insurance department.

Sales managers can also obtain bonuses from the dealership or the factory for meeting sales goals, figured either in dollars or number of units sold.

A dealership expression that has endured the test of time is: "Do the numbers and the dollars will take care of themselves." This means that if a dealership concentrates on sales volume, there will be lots of money at the end of the month regardless of profit made on any individual deal.

Later on, as you begin negotiating with sales managers, remember this expression when a sales manager insists that a low profit deal could not be considered. There are no experienced sales managers working today that do not know, understand, or embrace this expression.

Sales managers are busy people. Customers should not call Fridays, Saturdays or Mondays if they expect a good deal or a lot of the sales manager's time. Tuesdays and Wednesdays are normally slow, and managers will be wanting to deal.

Keep the annual and monthly cycles in mind, but don't hesitate to shop anytime you want or need a car. Use this book and you'll pay less than anyone would--anytime.

The Time of the month also has its influence:

Best Time---End of the month, right down to the last day of the month. Managers are usually doing anything possible to sell cars--even at "ridiculous" prices--in order to obtain volume bonuses.

Worst Time---First few days of the month. Dealers tend to be less negotiable starting a new month, and are not into the volume "swing" yet.

The time of year has limited influence. Most dealers are ready and willing to deal year around, although weather and new model-year introductions may have an impact. As a rule, dealers are more anxious when the weather is bad, and less anxious when the new models have just been introduced and are limited in availability, usually in the fall.

They are most anxious when they have many identical models in stock, and least anxious when they proudly own a hard-to-get, everybody wants'em, nobody's got 'em model. Even desirable colors can affect a dealers attitude toward selling.

SERVICE MANAGERS

Service managers are usually salaried, but may also receive a commission and bonuses on their department's overall profits.

They might manage, in larger stores, several service writ-ers, who deal directly with customers--making repair esti-mates, writing up service orders, seeing if any warranties are applicable, and the like.

The service departments' mechanics do three types of work. Two of them only earn the service department a dis-counted or wholesale rate for labor: **factory-authorized warranty work**, and **internal dealership work**, such as used-car reconditioning, so-called "dealer prep" and instal-lation of after-market products.

The third area is full-mark-up **retail service work**, which the service manager promotes in the local community. This is the most profitable type of service work, but be-cause the department is highly pressured into performing less-profitable internal and factory work first, the service manager must constantly perform a high-tension balancing act.

Obviously, service managers are in charge of a large profit center for the dealership, and in these economic times can mean the difference between being in, or out, of business.

Profits are large enough that an old rule-of-thumb, known as "service absorption," became part of dealership jargon. What it means is that the profits from the service department could cover the entire overhead costs of the dealership. This ideal, though now a rare situation, would make all car sales "gravy," or pure profit for the dealership.

Service managers have also become very important to the factory and the dealership in terms of product quality and customer satisfaction (which, as will be explained shortly, have become very important themselves), as well as for repeat business from customers.

In addition, service managers may be paid bonuses for maintaining high customer satisfaction ratings from new-car buyers.

Many factories have begun requiring the dealership sales person to introduce the service manager to the customer at

the time of the sale. Some even want customers to be given a tour of the service department when they buy new cars.

So, even though the service manager will not be involved in the negotiation of the car deal with the buyer, the service department now plays a crucial role for a dealership in keeping customers satisfied--and in getting them back into the dealership to buy their next cars.

FINANCE & INSURANCE MANAGERS

The finance and insurance (F&I) department is a back-end department like the service department. It offers the dealership the highest potential profit with the lowest actual overhead of any of the back-end departments. It has therefore become as crucial to a dealer's financial success as the service department.

F&I managers--also known as business managers, finance managers or some similar title--are the ones who do the "paperwork" on a new-car deal. Most importantly to the consumer, F&I managers are also sales people. They sell so-called "after-market" financial products, including payment plans (yes, these are "sold," and interest rates are not always automatic), extended service contracts (with pricing that is usually negotiable), credit life and disability insurance, among others.

They also may offer additional automotive products, although many large dealerships today have specialized accessory sales departments.

Usually, because of expert sales skills, it is the F&I manager who offers the customer undercoating, paint sealant, fabric protector, rust inhibitor, as well as accessories such as sunroofs and anti-theft systems.

They can sell everything, in short, from mud flaps to money.

It is the customer's money that is the major concern of F&I managers, since they are most often compensated on a commission-only basis.

GENERAL MANAGERS

The designated "heavy hitters" of dealerships are the general managers, who report to the owners or principals.

General managers are the pace setters of the business, responsible for the management and profitability of all sales and operational departments, and having final responsibility for ordering, negotiations and liaison with the factory.

Usually their personal income is based on some percentage of overall dealership profitability, although some salary might be included in a general manager's remuneration package. They seldom get involved with specific deals.

General managers should be viewed by the No-Enemies car buyer as a sort of "court of final appeal" if new-car sales managers prove unreceptive, insincere or intractable during negotiations.

2.   THE DEALERSHIP SELLING SYSTEM

The retail automobile business has been described as a
game with mismatched players. The dealership selling
system promotes this idea of car purchasing as a game.
Too often the competition--the enemy, if you will--is the
new-car buyer.

Confronting the dealer's team, which does its job 365
days a year, is usually an uninformed, unknowledgeable
and unconfident car buyer who has little chance of win-
ning.

If consumers believe that they won a great deal after purchasing a vehicle under the dealership system, they can be
sure of only one thing--that they did not get the best deal
they could have.

As in any sales endeavor, the very heart of the dealership
selling system beats with the idea that buyers usually will
not purchase any product or service unless their perception
of its value meets or exceeds its price. The effective sales
person, therefore, must create perceptions of tremendous
value in a customer's eyes, when in fact the value is small
or even non-existent in the product or service.

Value-building techniques are part and parcel of the sales
person's bag of tricks, including such things as "special
sales," "coupon savings", "act now" advertising blitzes and
free gifts, to name only a very few. The dealership selling
system is, in fact, a collection of such marketing, sales,
promotional and public relations techniques created to deliver an enhanced perception of value to the customer.

The No-Enemies Buying Method ignores these manipu-
lative methods, concentrating instead on helping consum-

ers buy the car they want at the best possible price--rather than doing battle with the dealership system and the sales person.

A typical car-shopping experience may include any combination of the following dealership system techniques.

☐ Dealers want to price their cars as high as possible so they can offer consumers discounts, rebates and trade-in allowances. New cars often sport "second stickers" on their

---

Car Sales Lingo

Grape/Guppy/Laydown/Flop-over---Are easy to sell and they buy anything you offer without negotiating.

Bustin' Bugs/Burnin' Gas---The customer is driving the new car as we speak. Often said to a banker who is trying to turn down the car loan; "But Bob, he's already bustin' bugs."

Puppy dog/Pull toy---Said of a customer who the sales person leads all over the lot because the customer cannot make up his mind. The reverse can be true, where the salesman follows the customer all over the lot like a puppy. Either use suggests that the sales person is ineffective.

Peddler---A car salesman.

Knee Deep in Rubber---The tires have a lot of tread left.

Tissue---Invoice or dealer cost. "A duce over tissue" means $200 over invoice.

Dip/Glue---Deposit from the customer that helps to hold a deal together. It can include a released title for a trade, etc.

Mouse the down---Have the customer borrow from a finance company to obtain the down payment.

Home Run/Big gross/Big hit/Swat/Slam Dunk---There was a big profit made on the deal.

For more car lingo, see Page 133

side windows, showing added dealer mark-up from the manufacturer's suggested retail price.

☐ Sales people will try to quickly find out all they can about car buyers in conversation, as much to determine their personality type and thus how to sell them, as to discover their preferences and financial status. These initial discussions often sound like job interviews or mortgage applications. How dealerships and sales people view the car-buying customer will be expanded upon in Chapter III.

☐ Sales people will try to keep customers ignorant of as many things as possible, staying away from details and specifics for as long the customer allows.

☐ As the sales process wears on, sales people will persistently suggest dealer financing, and present financing alternatives in "monthly payment-only" terms (see Chapter III), most often as though it is a natural or understood direction for buyers to follow.

☐ Sales people will go downstream with customers during sales discussions, leading them to believe that even impossible-to-deliver terms and incentives are attainable. That these pie-in-the-sky-promises do not exist is only broken to car buyers after they have fallen in love with the car.

☐ Sales people will try to get a commitment to purchase from the customer on the same day that they first appear on the dealership lot. Top-caliber sales people are masters at obtaining such commitments, especially when customers look like they're ready to leave the premises.

A favorite technique used is the "would-ya-take..." sales ploy, which involves gradual decreases in price, starting at the heavily marked-up retail sticker, until a figure is reached that customers will accept.

The price may or may not be acceptable to management, and in fact may be literally impossible to meet. But sales people are not concerned about that inconsistency; the point for them is to keep the customer on the lot.

As long as the customer remains on the lot, the sales person can continue to work the customer into making commitments. The final price will most likely be higher, and in many cases much higher, than the proffered "would-ya-take" amount.

☐ A "turnover," or TO, is another method sales people use to hold onto potential car buyers. It simply means that a customer is turned over from sales person to sales person, a proven method that can generate more profit per deal than any other for the dealer.

Some car buyers might deal with two or three different sales people, usually winding up with the sales manager or F&I manager.

The turnover system is calculated to wear down the customer the same way a battlefield commander might wear down an enemy by repeatedly attacking with fresh troops. Each sales person starts at the beginning with the customer searching for a new angle not exploited previously. If the customer stays on the lot long enough, each objection they have to making a deal will eventually become a casualty of the turnover system.

And be warned that along the way, profit-packed "up sell" items can be, and usually are, very smoothly added.

Some dealers might employ a variation on the turnover theme, using a two-person liner-closer method. The liner is a sales person who works with the customer until basic commitments are made, who then turns the buyer over to

the closer, a senior sales person or sales manager who puts
the deal in final form.

☐ Even when a customer leaves the lot, expert sales
people can get them to come back with a technique commonly referred to as "the bubble" or "low-line."

The method involves a sales person painting an appealing image of exactly what the buyer wants in a car, a price
or a monthly payment. "You can have that $25,000 luxury
sedan for only $250 a month." "That $16,000 red convertible sports car can be had for only ten grand," the sales person confidentially whispers. The image is most often pure
fantasy.

The customer, wary but floating on air, leaves the lot and
begins shopping specifically for a brand-new $16,000 red
convertible for $10,000. The customer drags himself back
in a week, after failing to find anything even in the same
ball park. The sales person promptly bursts the customer's
bubble. But the bubbled car buyer is safely back on the lot
and can be steered to some other purchase.

☐ Perhaps the most important psychological technique
used by car salesmen is to make the customer feel like a fool
when the customer is raising a valid concern.

For example, a salesman works the customer all afternoon and talks only about three-year loans. When it comes
time to negotiate, the customer declares, "I thought this
was a three-year loan, not a five-year loan." The salesman
looks at the customer as if he or she were stupid and says,
"How could we ever get a $300 payment on a three year
loan for this price of car?" And, the customer, feeling like a
fool, does not question him further, and fails to press the
issue. The truth here is the salesman has been plotting this
move all day.

☐   Another technique is called "spot delivery." Here the dealership gives the customer the car to take home and show his friends and neighbors, even though all of the paperwork details may not have been completed. The psychological advantage gained by spot delivery is "mental ownership." Such ownership is very powerful; once a buyer has shown his new car to family, friends and neighbors, he or she is unlikely to return it simply because the dealership has made a few "minor" financial adjustments.

An example: On a weekend a customer takes delivery of a new car and trades in the old car. The old car has $2,000 owing on it, the customer estimates based on a quick look at the payment book. The dealer uses this estimate, does all the paperwork, and delivers the new car to the customer. "We'll get the actual payoff on Monday," declares the finance manager.

Monday comes and $2,800 is owing, not $2,000. The dealer calls the customer asking for the $800 difference in cash. The customer does not want to give up the new car, not now with everyone admiring it--and he certainly does not want his old car back. He reluctantly forks over $800.

The $800 due is not the dealer's "fault", for the customer's estimate was used. However, had the car not been delivered on the spot, the likelihood is the deal would not have held together.

Most spot stores do not operate illegally, although some have been accused of "bashing" the customer after the sale. Bashing means substituting completely new terms, like a higher price for a car the customer has taken delivery days earlier.

Beware! The dealership system is designed to outwit the customer. If shoppers try to fight the dealership with traditional consumerist buying systems, it will marshall its well-trained forces and still win.

There are variations of all of these techniques, and many others besides. Any one of them should alert consumers that they are being manipulated by the dealership selling system.

If shoppers allow the dealership selling system to take control, they will be hearing about discounts from the sticker price, heavy emphasis on monthly payment amounts, and trade-in allowances.

The No-Enemies Method, alternatively, is a non-combative, knowledge-based methodology which gives the customer the choice of taking control of the car-purchasing process.

3. THE 21st CENTURY DEALERSHIP

Most American buyers may not know it yet, but the automobile industry is evolving into a new form.

Certainly, they are aware of the changes in society at large over the latter half of the 20th Century. Increased consumer activism, erosion of faith in American institutions, the import car invasion from Japan and almost continual economic uncertainties and disasters have had their effect everywhere, but nowhere more than with the auto trade.

What more American an institution, after all, and what more likely a product to fall prey to consumerism, foreign invasions and economic woes, than the American automobile?

There have been many attempts by car manufacturers and dealers to stem this tide. One of the more noticeable shifts is an emphasis on leasing. The industry is promoting the idea that leases are cheaper for the consumer, when often the reality is far different.

The car industry's current love affair with leases is an example of the types of schemes that treat symptoms rather than causes.

Not all leases are inappropriate, but it is enough to note here that in many cases where manufacturers aggressively promote leasing, the company is really trying to shorten the consumer's trading cycle--it wants consumers to purchase new vehicles more often.

There are changes being wrought in the car industry, however, which will have a more positive and permanent effect. These revolve around three major developments:

1. an increased emphasis on quality;

2. an increased emphasis on customer satisfaction;

3. delivery of actual value, rather than merely the perception of value.

Some consumers now recognize that car makers are doing more than just giving lip service to these now-entrenched concerns of the car-buying public. The necessity of meeting these concerns will not go away, either, as long as there is a consumer advocate left to draw breath or another country competing for the American car-buying dollar.

Unfortunately, some auto manufacturers are still bogged down by the traditional dealership sales system where dealers are not going to make great deals for the customer if they can help it. However, they will make such deals with consumers who have the knowledge and confidence necessary to negotiate such deals.

The No-Enemies Buying Method is one that consumers can use here and now to purchase a car at wholesale, or even below dealer cost with no stress before, during or after.

There are a number of parallel developments which assist the customer in applying the No-Enemies Buying Method.

☐ Consumers, after decades of education, are making it difficult for dealers to hold high profit margins, especially in new-car sales.

☐ The dealer cost for cars and trucks is high and growing higher, in many cases moving out of the affordable range of their customers--even without a retail mark-up. Since most dealers borrow the money to pay for their inventory of cars in stock, the carrying costs, or "flooring," is prohibitive if cars don't sell. This means dealers must move cars as quickly as possible to stay solvent.

☐ Customer loyalty to particular makes or models of cars is low due to the explosion in the number and types available to choose from. In 1990, car buyers had more than 60 automotive brands from which to choose.

☐ Over production of popular models by car manufacturers keeps their per-car production cost down.

☐ Manufacturers flood the market with used cars as a result of their buy-back of daily rentals. The manufacturers are guaranteeing buy-back to get the cars sold in the first place, due to over production. Known in the industry as "Program Cars", these are bought back by the manufacturers and flooded through the auctions nationwide for very cheap prices. Thus, a six-month-old program car might be available for $4,000 to $6,000 less than a new one. These

What Some Industry Authorities Are Saying About CSI

"The franchised new-vehicle dealership of the future will emphasize customer service and satisfaction."

L. Joseph Schmoke, President
University Consultants, Inc.
(Source: Automotive News, 1991)

"Customer service will rule the road in the '90s. It's clearly the most critical issue we face."

Keith Crain, Publisher & Editorial Director
Automotive News
(Source: Automotive News, 1991)

"For all of us in the automotive business, our quality and levels of consumer satisfaction will continue to drive our success in the 1990s. We are facing more competition than ever before, more product lines with increasing technology, higher product quality standards, and more customers that are very demanding. The differentiating factor will focus on satisfying the customer. Not just saying the words, but living with them."

Lee Miskowski, Vice President & General Manager
Ford Parts & Service Division
(Source: Automotive News, 1991)

practices make it more difficult for dealers to move higher-priced new cars off their lot.

☐ Worldwide economic and political realities have made consumers cautious when it comes to big-ticket spending.

☐ The most significant development is one that is part of the evolution of consumer-consciousness within the car industry itself--something known as CSI.

CSI stands for Customer Satisfaction Index, a system of rating dealerships by car manufacturers. These ratings, in essence, create a self portrait or report card. Some manufacturers use other acronyms, such as QCP (Quality Commitment Program).

These ratings are based on consumers' stated attitudes about the quality of the car they bought and the treatment they received at the dealership.

Most new-car buyers today receive a mail questionnaire from the manufacturer, usually within 30 days. It asks consumers questions about their new car, and how they were treated by dealership personnel. Later on, usually after six months or so, but within the first year of ownership, a follow-up survey asks similar questions, including some concerning the service department's quality of service.

When you see or hear a car company boast of its high customer-satisfaction ratings, on TV commercials or elsewhere, it is the result of these survey questionnaires.

These responses are tallied by the factory utilizing sophisticated computer programs.

Automobile manufacturers have spent millions researching customer satisfaction and developing these question-and-answer sheets. These surveys are vitally important to manufacturers.

The factories have determined that the more customers are satisfied with the quality of their new cars and how they were treated by the dealership, the higher the likelihood that customers will become repeat buyers. The higher the customer-satisfaction rating a car manufacturer receives, the higher the likelihood that car owners of competing makes will be drawn to its standard, as well.

Car manufacturers have realized that if they are to remain competitive in the 21st Century, customer satisfaction must become a top priority. It must become a top priority, as is the case with most American businesses today.

As stated by Newsweek magazine's "1990 Buyers of New Cars Summary Report," more than half (56 percent) of the 14,318 survey respondents said that their buying decisions were strongly influenced by manufacturer claims of being number one in customer satisfaction. This response was selected most often from a questionnaire written to determine the influence of advertising on customer buying.

Manufacturer studies indicate that car dealers would be more profitable if they increased their CSI ratings. Since CSI is important to the factory that supplies the cars to the dealership, CSI is important to the car dealership. Many car manufacturers today directly tie dealers' CSI performance to a number of criteria.

The nation's automobile grapevine is full of stories about priorities for best-selling car models going to the highest-performing CSI dealers. It is rumored that poor CSI performances cause dealers to get less-than-favorable treatment in everything from the flexibility and promptness of delivery schedules, to arranging an adequate supply of desirable inventory.

It is also said that new franchises or expansions have not been granted to some dealerships for the same reason. And, says the grapevine, the importance of CSI is increasing, and severe pressure is being brought to bear on dealers to meet high customer-satisfaction levels set by the factory.

Some dealers are very forthright and aggressive in a positive way about offering special things to their customers after they have bought their car--first oil change free, coupon books, special discounts on parts and labor, etc.

However, some dealers quietly imply that these nice things are in return for a good CSI rating. Although this practice is usually against factory rules, it is quite common. If you choose to accept these, you should not give the dealer undeserving high marks on the survey if, indeed, the treatment you received was less than good. On the other hand, if you have been treated well, the same sense of fairness demands that you take the time to fill out the questionnaire and grade the dealer accordingly.

The Customer Satisfaction Index, born of the economic realities of the 20th Century, will do more to evolve the practices and attitudes of the 21st Century dealership than any other single development.

Already, some more enlightened dealership sales managers have been known to reject high-profit deals presented to them by salesmen because they were concerned that the customer would not respond favorably to a CSI survey!

Further, CSI has begun to change the dealership sales system to the degree that low-profit deals are becoming an accepted way of doing business. Building relationships with customers at all levels of the dealership is starting to be seen by these dealers as more profitable than beating a customer with the dealership sales system.

Some experts view the 21st Century dealership as having salaried consultants demonstrating vehicles, rather than traditional commissioned sales people. Saturn is already trying a variation of this theme.

The No-Enemies Buying Method gives consumers the means to contribute to the changes occurring in the industry. It replaces the existing factors of the dealership sales system--manipulation, uncertainty and competition--with mutual respect, knowledge and understanding.

Saturn: A No-Enemies Company

As introduced in this book, auto manufacturers are taking great pains to keep customers satisfied. Among others, companies like Toyota and Lexus, Mercedes Benz, Cadillac, Lincoln, Infiniti, Acura and Honda have earned reputations for being consistently high in customer satisfaction and product quality. In addition to Cadillac and Lincoln, other "domestics" are making excellent strides as well.

One interesting company that can be analyzed for this example is Saturn. A subsidiary of General Motors, Saturn is as much an experiment for GM, as it is a car company.

Some day historians may focus their attention on Saturn. If it no longer builds cars, they are likely to conclude that Saturn was too nice to its customers.

If, because of this sensitivity to customer's desires, it prospers and changes the industry, it will be credited with the foresight to synchronize its culture with the changes brought about by the CSI (Customer Satisfaction Index) revolution.

One of the most dramatic pieces of evidence regarding Saturn's CSI orientation came very early in Saturn's business life, when it recalled 1,836 cars because of an improperly formulated engine coolant from the coolant manufacturer. 1,100 of these were already in the hands of customers. Instead of cutting corners, as they could have done with such a minor repair, Saturn completely replaced the cars for the customers.

This move was applauded by both automotive experts and customers.

But, Saturn goes further. It offers an unconditional 30-day or 1500-mile money back guarantee. If you don't like the car for any reason, return it--no questions asked. One Saturn sales manager tells a story of a customer returning a Saturn because he did not like the color. The customer got the color desired--no questions asked. It is Saturn's policy that buyers can get a replacement car, or even their money back.

Saturn is marketing to middle America, offering cars in the $10,000 range, and has a very low mark-up as compared with industry averages. The sticker price mark-up varies from approximately $300 to $1500. Further, Saturn pays no hold-back, offers no factory rebates, has no fleet sales or pro-grammed buy-back of cars to dilute resale values. (Holdback and buy-backs will be described later in the book.)

Saturn sales people are generally not paid on the gross profit of a sale, because the mark-up is so low. They are usually paid a fixed amount per car (a flat commission) regard-less of profit attained. Bonuses are normally paid on the number of units sold. Saturn sales managers say this enables sales people to be more like consultants. The remuneration system puts an emphasis on product value and customer service, and allows a very soft approach to sales.

Saturn will soon be launching a new, two-part program that will create a more personal and intimate relationship between the factory, on one hand, and both customers and dealership employees, on the other.

Under the first part of the program, the factory employees drive home the automobiles as they are built. That way, the people who built the car can see if there are any bugs in its manufacture--before the car gets delivered to the dealer.

Saturn will closely monitor the one-day use of the cars, making sure it has only been driven to and from home by the worker, and that less than 100 miles is put on the odometer.

Workers, as a result, will be able to critique, and feel responsible for their own workmanship. In addition, their comments
will be used to improve the product.

Once the car, driven by the worker, is purchased by a
customer, the worker will telephone the customer, introduce
himself and chat about the quality of the car.

The second part of the program involves factory workers
becoming closer to the dealers. Each Saturn dealer around
the country is, in effect, adopted by a factory worker. The
worker calls the dealership's managers on a frequent basis to
answer questions and help with any problems that arise.

Saturn is, thus, attempting to bridge the notorious gap
between the "big, bad factory" and the people who receive
their cars. They are attempting, in a very progressive way, to
put a face behind the name.

The biggest question in the Saturn experiment, especially
in light of the corporation's "currently in-the-red status", is
whether Saturn can be profitable or not. Sure, it is nice to be
nice, but a company can't be nice if it is out of business.

Regardless of how things turn out for Saturn, it is an
experiment conceived out of respect for the customer. If
anyone believes that CSI is not important to car manufacturers, they should consider Saturn.

CHAPTER III

THE NEW-CAR BUYER

The first two chapters of this book have been about change. They have introduced the No-Enemies Buying Method and discussed the evolutionary changes in the car industry that has allowed it to come into being. It builds friendly relations with car dealers that will save money now and in the future for consumers, yet also keeps dealers in business during these tough economic times.

The one thing basic to the car-buying process that has not changed is that the customer must pay for the car. The various methods of financing a car are few and predictable--so predictable that as soon as experienced sales people identify a customer's financing options, they will quickly pattern their sales techniques to match the advantages and disadvantages inherent in those options.

Terminology may differ among sales people around the country, but generally speaking, they group consumers into four major financing categories:

1. **True cash**, or **cash-difference, buyers**--consumers who can finance a new-car purchase with cash out of their own pocket, with or without a trade-in.

2. **One-pay cash buyers**--customers who finance a new-car purchase through their own bank or credit union.

3. **Payment buyers**--consumers who shop for cars with the size of the monthly payment as their main criterion.

4. **Captive buyers**--"unfinanceable" for one reason or another, who need the dealer's help to qualify for a car loan.

Once a buyer can be placed in one of these categories, the sales person or sales manager can apply different sales techniques to close a deal on a car. There are subtle differences in technique, but the end result will invariably be the same--high-profit for the dealership--unless the car buyer is familiar with the ploys used by dealers in setting up financing arrangements, and how they will affect the cost of the car they want to purchase.

Cash Buyer. . . .

The first category, from a customer's point of view, is the best one. A cash buyer is one of the toughest of all customers to sell from the sales person's perspective. This is primarily because they are using their own hard-earned money to make the purchase.

It could also be because their credit ratings are so stellar that they can easily make financing arrangements without the aid of the dealership. A buyer who can immediately write a check, even if it is a line of credit check, is considered a cash buyer,

Car sales people sometimes refer to them as "slow-breathers" or "bottom-line buyers" who are tough to get an immediate commitment from. Since they have cash-in-hand, most true cash buyers are slow to part with it unless truly convinced they are getting a good "cash" deal. This group tends to shop around, as much because they do not buy cars very often as because they want to protect their money.

Sales people see cash buyers with "low-profit deal" written all over them, not only because such consumers seek big discounts on new cars, but because they will want more money for trade-ins than a dealer could offer wholesale.

One-pay cash buyer. . . .

One-pay cash buyers are similar in their shopping habits to cash buyers, except that they must use someone else's cash to pay for a car purchase, usually arranged through a bank or a credit union. They are still difficult sales prospects for dealerships, because cash buyers of any sort make it difficult for sales people to control the deal.

The one-pay cash buyer may masquerade as a true cash buyer, even though they have not yet actually arranged their financing. This deception may enable them to drive a hard bargain and get a better price than they could without it, but that is their only advantage. Effectively, all it accomplishes is to make the buyer as devious as the sales people.

It is not necessary that consumers misrepresent themselves to get a good deal on a car. The No-Enemies Buying Method--again, simply based on customer knowledge, confidence and responsibility--not only will bring a much better financial deal today for the one-pay cash buyer, but will build a good relationship with the dealership for the future.

Payment buyers. . . .

The third type of car buyer, the payment buyer, more than makes up for any problems that true cash or one-pay cash buyers create for dealership sales forces.

Payment buyers use "convenient" dealer financing even though most could probably go to a bank or credit union and arrange a car loan by themselves. They often blindly elect dealer financing without shopping around for lenders. The reasons why they don't could be lack of knowledge, or even an unreasonable fear of the process.

Payment buyers are, in any case, responsible for the greatest portion of profits for car dealers.

The difference is that payment buyers are shopping not only for a car but for a monthly payment plan that will suit their budgets. The latter can often be more important to the payment buyers than any other aspect of a deal, including the price of the car or trade-in value.

Sales people and F&I managers welcome them with open arms, since payment buyers give dealerships the best opportunity to make a profit, not only on the sale price of a car but also on payment plans and the various after-market products and services. Once payment buyers fix a certain car and a monthly payment amount in their heads, they open themselves up to every trick of the car trade.

A sales person or F&I manager can easily add $2,000 to a deal, as long as they keep the monthly payment amount near what the buyer has envisioned. It is easy to see that $19 a month sounds better than $1,000 in cash, when really they might be roughly equivalent.

Payment buyers often appear oblivious to the total cost of a car deal. They seem not to care, for example, that a $200 monthly payment would cost only $4,800 over 24 months, but $12,000 over 60 months. Even hardened F&I managers are amazed at the frequency with which payment buyers ask how much they actually will be paying for their cars--after they've signed the contracts!

Captive buyers. . . .

Captive buyers are those with poor credit histories, are first-time car buyers who have not yet established credit, or are virtually anyone who cannot finance a car without a dealer's help. These buyers traditionally have the least control over financing terms, and who usually pay the most.

They literally have no recourse. Car dealers do; in fact, "recourse" is an important part of their financial arsenal. What recourse means is that a dealer chooses to guarantee payment of a loan to a local bank for a captive buyer. Since the dealer, in effect, becomes the captive buyer's co-signer, higher profits will normally be sought to cover that greater risk.

This is simply a fact of business life: those who take higher risks in any financial deal, from buying stock to selling cars, believe they are entitled to the potential of higher rewards.

Certainly, car dealers are entitled to at least protect themselves against potential losses should buyers not keep up with payments or otherwise fail to honor a contract. Just as certain, captive buyers with a history of credit problems have the least chance of making any deal at all for a car purchase, much less a rock-bottom deal. Any inability to make payments in the past--and often merely the lack of a credit history--has a chilling effect on financing in the present.

No-Enemies captive buyers will be very relieved to know that they need not be held a captive to this state of affairs if they understand a few basic facts.

Most people are not anxious to divulge their lack of credit, poor credit histories or past financial problems, since they think it will negatively affect their chances of making a deal. What has a truly negative effect is when captive buyers lie about their financial situation.

Experienced sales people immediately see a red flag when they hear car buyers make certain apparently innocent statements. Those who openly claim they "have no credit problems", "don't even like credit", "cut up their credit cards years ago" or even "just qualified for a mortgage" are warning salesmen to look at their credit history closely.

Dealership personnel realize that the only people who honestly have tried not to use credit are usually young, first-time car buyers who haven't applied for credit yet. The personnel of well managed dealerships view dimly misrepresentation by consumers, and get angry and insulted when they get "taken down the garden path" themselves by customers representing themselves as qualified car buyers who in fact are not.

The first rule, therefore, for every customer who has credit today, should be to check and correct at least annually the credit reports prepared by any of the following agencies:

CBI---The Credit Bureau, Inc./Equifax

TUCI---TransUnion Credit Information

CCS---Chilton Creditmatic Systems

TRW---TRW Credit Information Services

ASC---Associated Credit Services

These agencies compile customer credit reports for banks, department stores, auto dealerships--anywhere consumers use credit. Consumers may contact these organizations to obtain a copy of their credit report. They should look under "credit reporting agencies" in the Yellow Pages.

For consumers who wish to continually monitor their credit ratings, there are two excellent aids available today.

One is from CBI/Equifax, called **Financial Update** (1-800-777-0440). Every three months, for an annual fee of $34.95, Equifax sends subscribers an updated credit report and analysis. Free copies of a customer's complete credit report are available at any time, upon request, as well as a list of any and all outside inquiries.

The second, **TRW's Credentials Service** (1-800-262-7432), costs between $20 and $39 annually, depending on the type of services desired. TRW will send a copy of a customer's credit report at no extra charge, on request, and will send notice of any inquiries.

Contact these companies for complete information on these programs.

Consumers with no credit or poor credit, meanwhile, would do best by being up-front about the facts when buying a car.

Unfortunately, at least one consumerist car-buying method advises to the contrary, suggesting that consumers pretend that they have no credit problems. The rationale offered was that, once dealers have invested time and effort in selling a car, they will get a deal financed, no matter what the customer's credit situation.

From the seasoned car person's perspective, this is simply ludicrous. Dealerships are members of the credit agencies listed above, and literally have instant access to a customer's credit report through their computer systems. Once customers sign a credit application, they are literally "found out" within minutes--even on Sundays.

The reality is that honesty is the best policy. Car people are far more apt to respect and, indeed, help customers who have been honest about their credit history.

Dealerships expect to see customers with credit problems, more today than ever before. They are ready and willing to bend-over-backward to gain financing for customers who have simply told them the true nature of their financial situation. The captive buyer with credit problems can still gain bank financing, even if the dealer has no recourse but to go to "recourse."

Recourse, known in the car business as "kissing the paper", simply means that a lender has someone to fall back on, other than the customer, to recover its funds should a loan go into default. Most dealers do not actually make loans to customers. Dealers are merely intermediaries between the customer and a lending institution.

Because of a potential or actual credit risk with the marginal credit customer, lenders sometimes require dealers to take a more active financial position. Recourse defines that position, identifying the degree of responsibility a dealer has for a customer loan on a new-car purchase.

The No-Enemies Buying Method provides this information about recourse loans to enable captive buyers to better evaluate the deal and what the sales manager is saying about recourse. As a result the buyer will gain respect--not to mention a great deal on a car.

There are several different types of recourse loans:

Non-recourse loans: Also known as WOR (without recourse), if a customer fails to pay off a loan, the bank has no recourse but to have the car repossessed, and the car then belongs to the bank.

Because the risk is the bank's, only customers with good credit ratings, stable jobs and sufficient down payments will qualify. Many dealers will only sell cars on a non-recourse basis.

Contrary to popular belief, many buyers with marginal credit are often closer to qualifying for financing than they know, a fact an unscrupulous dealer will conceal, leaving the customer feeling dependant on the dealer.

Unscrupulous dealers have been known to gouge marginal buyers by making them feel like second class citizens who have no other means of buying a car.

Co-signing, another method of establishing non-recourse to the dealer through a financially sound third party, has fallen out of favor with most banks, since they discovered that most co-signers who promise to repay loans seldom do so.

Full-recourse loans: Also known as an unconditional guarantee, or "UG", the full-recourse loan holds the dealer totally responsible for loan repayment if the customer defaults.

The dealer can even be charged for repossession costs and other collection-related fees.   Dealers, for obvious reasons, seldom consider arranging this type of a loan, even if it means losing a high-profit deal.

Limited recourse loans: There are two types of limited recourse, or "LR" financing instruments: **90-day recourse,** and **dollar guarantees**.   The more common of the two, the 90-day recourse loan requires the dealer to pay off the customer's loan only if the bank recovers and returns the car to the dealership lot within 90 days of the loan's delinquency.

The other limited recourse loan type involves dollar guarantees, which began gaining popularity in the '80s because dealers could know their total exposure up front. These agreements require the dealer to pay the bank a fixed, predetermined amount, generally between $200 and $1,000, in the event of a repossession.

Dollar guarantees are usually used to help arrange financing for customers with good credit ratings who might not have a sufficient down-payment to meet bank guidelines for a non-recourse loan, often because they owe large amounts for outstanding loans on their trade-ins.

*   *   *

Most car buyers with no or poor credit, but armed with sufficient funds for a down-payment and the No-Enemies Buying Method, can secure a car loan with the help of the dealer, plus a little common sense. That could translate not only into a new car but a brand-new or re-established credit rating.

Alternately--and probably before talking to dealers about their financial situation--car buyers with real or potential credit problems should be talking to their own bank or credit union officer and the credit reporting agencies listed above. This latter course affords consumers not only an estimate of their chances for getting a new car, but also the possibility of arranging financing and fixing their credit problems in the same afternoon.

Those without a banking or credit union relationship may face a little more work; but after all, what's a good credit rating worth today? If nothing more, it is worth the time to read the following.

THE NO-ENEMIES' CAPTIVE BUYER CHECKLIST

Consumers with poor, marginal or no credit, who lack a strong banking or credit union relationship, should take the following steps to improve their chances of getting a loan.

1. Obtain a copy of your credit report.

2. Shop banks or credit unions to find one that works on a recourse basis with local dealerships. If some do not, ask for referrals to ones that do. Do not fill out or sign loan or credit applications all over town. Each time you do this, an "inquiry" is submitted to credit reporting agencies, and too many inquiries make lenders nervous.

3. Package yourself for bankers. This means making available credit reports, income and employment verifications, credit references, rent or mortgage payment receipts to establish length of residency and prompt payment record, and any other positive financial information available. Try every way legally possible to gain a sufficient sum of money to be applied toward a down payment. Then make an appointment to see a banker.

4. Ask the chosen banker if a non-recourse loan is possible, or if any other banks might consider it. Ask if there are any circumstances whereby you might be financed on your own merit--a large down payment, for example. If the answer is yes, proceed with the No-Enemies Buying Method.

5. If the answer is no, then ask the banker for local dealerships who work with recourse buyers. Also inquire what to expect in terms of down payment, acceptable price ranges of cars likely to be approved for recourse loans, and the maximum loan term and monthly payments that could be expected. Then head for the dealership.

6. Ask to see the dealership's sales manager. Explain that a good deal is desired on a car, but that there have been credit problems. Highlight whatever strong points there are, the same ones presented to the banker.

7. If the sales manager is agreeable, fill out a credit application, discuss price ranges, cash down and payment plans that are feasible. Then ask the sales manager to call

in the loan application to the lender. If approved, continue on with the No-Enemies Buying Method.

8. If not approved, ask if other options are possible.

*   *   *

If intimidation is attempted, or if it becomes obvious that games are being played, you should not hesitate to leave. Most sales managers who are even minimally aware of general economic conditions and customer satisfaction will listen and discuss options.

Sales managers will be even more inclined along those lines if the buyer is talking their language and appears knowledgeable, confident and, in the case of recourse deals, responsible.

CHAPTER IV

STEP #1: GATHERING INFORMATION AND CHOOSING A CAR

One of the greatest shortcomings of car buyers is lack of knowledge. That is not surprising. There is so much to know about car dealerships and financing that even educated consumers might be unaware of much of the material in the preceding chapters and the rest of this book.

Buyers, thus, are often in the dark. And, when , in the blink of an eye, a sales pitch turns to talk of trade-in allowances, monthly payments and commitments, they become blinded by the dealership selling system.

The No-Enemies Buying Method sheds some much needed light on these subjects by providing buyers with the tools to find out exactly what they have and what they want.

Not knowing the details of the value of their trade-in or what they want in a new car, customers are apt to buy the car the dealer wants to sell them, and to take whatever is offered on their trade-in.

Step #1 of the No-Enemies Buying Method seeks to remedy that situation. This is the Age of Information; information abounds. The problem is finding good information that can be relied upon in making car-buying decisions. Fortunately, current technology has provided a new-car pricing service. An unimaginable concept only a few years ago, the pricing service provides what once was "insider-only" information.

Accurate dealer cost information is an absolute necessity when buying a car today. That knowledge provides confidence that the customer will be treated with honesty. The No-Enemies Buying Method can hardly work without such information; the lack of it appreciably reduces the method's effectiveness, makes the buying process more time-consuming, and returns an element of control to the car dealership system.

A call to a new-car pricing service provides an accurate quote of the current dealer cost and suggested retail price comparisons of most cars and trucks on the market today.

Other highly detailed information--standard and optional equipment, for example, and available factory rebates and incentives--is usually included. Optional equipment and equipment packages are complicated to sort out these days, so this service is especially helpful to car buyers.

Shoppers can obtain access to a pricing service from a number of sources. Generally, there are three ways a company or organization provides this service to consumers.

1. For a price per printout, usually $11 to $14, via an 800 number with credit card or written order.

2. Through the use of 900 numbers, where the information is delivered verbally at a cost per minute that ranges from $1.50 to $3.

3. Printouts or verbal dealer cost information is provided free of charge by member organizations like credit unions, or by companies offering cost information as only a complementing feature of their main consumer or member service.

Although this buying method does not endorse the use of 900 numbers to provide this service, it does not mean those companies are less than credible. Customers electing the "1-900" option for time saving convenience or otherwise are advised to check carefully the rates and services offered by each company.

Options 1 and 3 are excellent ways to obtain the information. Consumer Reports offers cost printouts for $11 per quote, and similar offerings are made by companies like AAA, USAA, as well as many of the travel clubs nationwide. Contact these organizations about actual details and prices.

One of the best sources is your local credit union, if they indeed offer this service. Many credit unions are now offering step-saving services to members, with loan pre-approoavals, free dealer cost information, as well as access to automotive industry magazines and publications to help their members select a vehicle. Hand-in-hand with the one-stop credit union concept, my company, U.S. Car Buying Service, gives out free dealer cost information on a limited basis when consumers elect either the "how-to" shopping package, or actual car buying service.

These two consumer services are described in detail in Chapter X--The Other Choice.

The new pricing advisories can be helpful immediately to anyone who wants to know whether or not a certain car is within their financial ball park, and is the first place consumers should go when looking for a car, if for no other reason that the time-savings involved. The last place buyers should go when deciding on the car they want is usually the first place they think they should go--to the car dealership.

Long before they need to be there, consumers get caught up in financial considerations and negotiations for "hot" cars that the sales people assure them won't be there if they leave the lot for more than five minutes.

At this point, consumers shouldn't be thinking about purchasing, pricing, down payments, loan programs or trade-in allowances. Right now, all a car shopper needs to focus on is answering one simple question: What car do I really want to own?

Step #1 only requires the buyer to chose one or a few car models that can be narrowed down later on. Interestingly, most people seem to automatically look only to vehicles they think they can afford.

However, because the No-Enemies Method can put cars that are considerably more expensive within reach, the conscious criteria should be primarily those of preference rather than price range. Buyers shouldn't be afraid to include cars that they may think "out of their league;" succeeding steps will automatically adjust those considerations.

There are ways, other than those mentioned earlier, of getting the information necessary to make these choices. Car shoppers could begin by talking to friends, neighbors and relatives about their cars. Don't worry about how

Retail versus invoice buying

By becoming invoice-plus buyers, consumers may find the "prices" of cars in different luxury classes much closer than expected:

	1991 Ford Escort **4-door hatch-back, LX**	**1991 Ford Taurus** **4-Door Sedan, L**
	Retail	**Invoice**
Standard	$9,136	$12,054
Destination Charges	375	490
Options	3,330	none
Total	**$12,841**	**$12,544**
	*48 monthly payments of $319	*48 monthly payments of $314

Using No-Enemies invoice-plus buying rather than sticker price retail buying, a base model Taurus can be purchased at less than the sticker price of a well equipped Escort.

Although many buyers would not prefer a moderately equipped Taurus, others would be thrilled to own a car that is two luxury classes higher--moderately equipped or not.

The difference between many manufacturers' retail and invoice prices for their lower and higher luxury model classes may be much closer than many consumers might realize.

This phenomenon allows No-Enemies car buyers to shop for models they previously perceived as "too expensive" because of high sticker prices.

* Calculated at 11%, assuming customer finances amount in the total column for each vehicle. Payment rounded to nearest dollar.

much they paid, for you will probably pay thousands less. Observe cars on the road and in parking lots--even dealers' lots, after they close.

Buyers with a research orientation may use any number of car magazines, and most daily newspapers have automotive sections that discuss the plusses and minuses of the different makes and models of cars on the market.

Consider what options you would like, such as the kind of radio or other product accessories. If there is a very strong preference for a particular model, it likely can be rented for a day from a car rental agency.

Car shopping should be fun! It certainly should not be a tedious and torturous experience overburdened by financial considerations--which is what many consumer advocate buying systems seem to encourage from the outset. Now's the time to fall in love with a car, as long as the emotion doesn't get in the way of negotiations later on.

When the choices for a new car are narrowed down to one or a few models it is time to visit the dealerships to pick up the product-line brochures on each model. The necessity for this is twofold:

1. The brochures will help narrow the car hunt further, and,

2. The brochures provide the very specific information needed later in negotiations concerning make, model, exterior and interior colors, options and equipment packages.

Beware, for as soon as anyone walks into a dealership, they represent a potential sale to a sales person. When a customer sets foot onto the showroom floor or lot, he or she customer sets foot onto the showroom floor or lot, he or she immediately becomes an "up"--the next turn at bat, so to speak, for the sales person next in line.

The best way for a brochure-seeking buyer to head them off is with five little words: "I am not an up." This polite phrase, which tells the sales person that the customer is speaking their language, also does them the courtesy of not wasting their time.

It also implies that the customer is familiar with the car business and not ready yet to make a purchase. If the salesman persists, merely explaining matters further will usually work.

This small assertion usually will allow consumers to be left alone in the dealership to pick up some product-line brochures. Moreover, it prevents consumers from becoming a particular sales person's proprietary customer if they return to the same dealership to buy a car. This freedom will be very important later on.

The No-Enemies Buying Method suggests that buyers directly approach the sales manager when ready to buy a car.

If buyers have not already opened discussions with sales people, that leaves sales managers free to make decisions--such as whether or not to use a sales person and pay a commission on the deal.

What if you are already working with a salesman, or have a friend or relative from whom you have purchased cars over the years? Out of courtesy, the method suggests that you continue to work with that sales person--if that person is indeed a friend, he or she will be glad to work the deal exactly the way you want it. Keep in mind that if the deal is not right, the sales managers at competing dealerships can be contacted using the method. And, wouldn't your friend want you to get the best deal?

Step #1 seems very simple, but the simple things are often taken for granted as understood. Their simplicity does not lessen their importance; the right beginning is always important in any endeavor. It might well be worth the few minutes it will take to go over this step again before moving on to Step #2.

Happy car hunting!

CHAPTER V

STEP #2: EVALUATING A TRADE-IN

American consumers are known for falling in love with their cars, and the romance nowhere is more obvious than when it comes time to say good-bye.

This combination of sentimentality, pride and financial expectation over a trade-in leaves people in a highly charged emotional state, especially if they've already fallen in love with a new car. Some buyers become absolutely unglued when presented a low trade-in value for their car, while others may be ecstatic with a high bid.

Sales people, meanwhile, have a very unemotional reason for making trade-in offers of any amount: to make the highest possible profit on the new-car sale.

The No-Enemies Buying Method suggests that buyers delay involving their emotions until after they have purchased their new car. If consumers really want to be happy when they drive their new car out of the dealer's lot, it behooves them to understand what happens when they drive in with their old one.

Consider the two completely opposite reactions to trade-in values quoted above. Both consumers, the happy one and the unhappy one, may have brought in identical cars, but received different trade-in allowances. The reason has to do with how the sales people intend to structure the new-car deal with the buyer. The difference in trade-in value happened because, in one case, the customer received an actual cash value (ACV) quote, while in the other a more generous "over-allowance" was presented.

Actual cash value represents how much a trade-in is worth to the dealership, as determined by the dealership appraiser, usually the used-car manager. This amount is always wholesale, and is usually close to what would be paid at an auto auction. Some appraisers rely on a variety of books that publish trade-in values, but used-car managers often will let the actual cash value be governed by the local market value of the car.

The actual cash value is computed by subtracting reconditioning costs (repairs, etc.) and the generous dealer mark-up (average gross profit) from the retail price a similar car would fetch on the used-car lot. For example:

$6,450 Retail selling price of trade-in

-1,500 Average gross profit

- 200 Reconditioning

4,750

- 250 Margin for error/hidden repairs

$4,500 Actual cash value (wholesale value) of trade-in

The trade-in allowance a customer receives can be lower than (under-allowance), equal to or higher than the actual cash value (over-allowance).

When sales people make customers happy by offering them more than the actual cash value, rest assured that there is more than enough profit in the deal to cover that over-allowance.

On paper, an over-allowance deal based on the above example looks like this to the customer:

$15,000 Retail price of new car

- 6,500 Trade-in allowance [Wow!]

$ 9,500 Selling price of new car to customer

The dealer has given the customer $2,000 more than actual cash value for the trade-in, and a selling price well below sticker, both of which makes the customer very happy.

The dealer, meanwhile, is even happier, since an enormous profit has been made on the deal.

After the deal is closed, the dealership calculates the deal this way:

$15,000 Selling price of new car

-10,000 Dealer cost (invoice from factory)

- 2,000 Trade-in over-allowance ($6,500 less $4,500)

$ 3,000 Gross profit to dealer [Wow!]

The dealer in fact is probably making even more on the deal, and this will be discussed later. The reality is that the $3,000 gross profit for the dealer also represents a huge overpayment for the buyer.

The customer, in this case, has paid too much--much too much--for that new car. The No-Enemies Buying Method prevents such overpayments.

It does this first by using only the actual cash value as a basis when figuring trade-in allowances at the dealer-

ship where the new car will be bought. Anything else is
just smoke and mirrors used by the dealership to convince the buyer of a great deal that really isn't.

Step #2, like all the other steps of the No-Enemies Buying Method, gives the customer choices. The choice here
involves how to sell the old car:

☐   As a trade-in at actual cash value to the new-
car dealer where the new car will be purchased;

☐   To another new-car dealer or a used-car dealer
at wholesale price;

☐   Or privately to another customer at a retail price.

The starting point, in any case, is to professionally clean
the used car (known in the industry as detailing) and make
any necessary minor repairs. Detailing does more to bring
a good price or trade-in allowance than most consumers
realize. It's like painting a house before selling it; the
cosmetic change adds value in the eyes of the buyer.

A new paint job for a used car is not on the list, however
(except for minor touch-ups), since cost and quality considerations probably make it prohibitive. Neither is re-
placing a transmission, adding a full set of tires or other
major repairs. A dealer can accomplish such things very
inexpensively; consumers cannot, unless they can do it
themselves.

So major overhauls are not recommended; but a good
cleaning is. This includes compounding, buffing and wax-
ing the exterior finish, as well as shining up tires and
whitewalls with a cleaning agent; steam-cleaning an exces-
sively dirty engine; shampooing or at least vacuuming the
interior, including the trunk, and treating vinyl and leather
surfaces; and getting a grease job and oil change, making

sure all other fluids (power steering, brake fluids, anti-freeze, Freon, etc.) are clean and at capacity.

Believe it or not, such detailing, including adding trim and stripes, white walling and even adding spoke wheel covers, can be done for less than $200. Set that $200 amount as a maximum for complete reconditioning expense, including any repairs, then get out the Yellow Pages and look under various headings such as "Auto Detailing" or "Auto Repair" to find companies or individuals who provide these services.

Approach them professionally, speaking their language, and seek wholesale or "dealer cost" prices. A car person's line of introduction might be something like, "Listen, I'm prepping my car to get some bids. Can you suggest what I can do--and can you give me dealer cost--on some "cheapie" (inexpensive) stuff that would give it good "eye-ball" (make it look more appealing).

The key is to spend as little money as possible to make the car in question look as good as possible. Understand, too, that dealers might pay only $50 or $75 for full detailing in their own shop, and maybe a little more if they go to an outside vendor. So stay comfortable, confident and shop around. Some local car washes offer a quick, good looking detail for only $20 to $30. Always elect their top-of-the-line service.

When prepping has been completed, "shop" the used car among wholesalers (new and used-car dealers), or try to sell it to a private party. The purpose now is only to collect bids and discover the maximum dollar value of the used car. Ignore, for the moment, any money still owed for loans outstanding on the used car. That factor doesn't figure in until the used car is actually sold, which doesn't happen here in Step #2.

The appraisals from wholesalers will vary literally all over the lot. Some will try to "steal" the trade by "lowballing" the customer, while others will "step up" and offer competitive pricing. How competitive they are will be discovered during negotiations with the new-car dealer. For now, the idea is just to see what's out there.

Often, the best places to obtain a generous bid are the new-car dealerships that sell the same make of car as the used one; some will be interested, and some won't, depending on market conditions at the time, or the volume of their used car sales.

A few phone calls to the used car managers at such dealerships will disclose which dealers are willing to discuss buying the used car.

Under no circumstances should consumers mention that they have intentions of using the proceeds of the sale when buying a new car--unless they want to listen to a sales pitch for another used car, and maybe even wind up talking to a new-car salesman.

Also, shoppers should not ask for a bid over the phone-- appraisers simply will not bid on a car without seeing it.

Used-car managers are master negotiators, experts in the business of buy-and-sell. If they ask how much is expected for the used car, consumers should explain that they'd rather see the manager in person to "put a number" on the car.

Used-car sales managers usually have very busy schedules, so the customer should acknowledge that and ask for a specific time to come in and visit. The reception, if they agree to meet, will be much warmer than if the customer shows up "cold" on the lot.

Use the same honest and open approach as well with each used-car dealer visited. Tell them the car is being "shopped" to get the best possible bid. Be proud of the car being offered to them; tell them of its quality over the phone and show them the well-detailed proof of it when meeting them face-to-face.

The wholesalers might want to know about things like the model, color, optional equipment, and mileage before they see it, so consumers should be prepared with as much information about the used car as possible.

Stay cool, control those emotions, and deliver only the facts asked for, accentuating the positives of the car along the way.

The purpose here is to get at least three firm bids from wholesalers, a price they will promise to pay for the used car. Consumers might be surprised when dealers try to get commitments to sell immediately, but this is not unusual. Commitment should not be made at this point; it should be simply stated the decision about selling the used car will be made within a few days.

Regardless of how much the bids vary, remember that dealers are street-smart negotiators who could try to rene-gotiate their bids. Chances are they won't do that if the seller remains confident and professional in approaching the deal.

Consumers might want to try to sell their used cars at retail to private parties, either themselves or through con-signment lots. Consignment lots generally agree to sell a car for a percentage or the selling price, or for a fixed amount above the selling price. Consignment lots, however, tend to be inconsistent as far as how well they move cars. Often the commission they charge outweighs their advantages even if the car does sell. If considering a consignment lot, consumers are advised to select carefully.

Consumers can also try to sell their used cars through the newspaper classified section, or to friends or relatives. This last option is strongly recommended, if the customer has the time, energy and patience to do so, and is willing to spend the money on advertising.

Both the consignment lot and the private-sale options require that the customer know what retail price the used car will fetch on the open market, which requires a bit more research. Comparable cars advertised in classified ads will also help establish a selling price, as will used-car price guides such as the NADA book, the Kelley Blue Book, and the Black Book.

Although retailing the used car privately makes it likely that a customer will get the best possible price, it is almost impossible to control the timing of such deals. The buyer might want to take possession of the used car before consumers are ready to buy their own new cars, or they might delay or back out of the deal at the last minute.

Bids from wholesalers have the advantage of being completely unemotional and more or less guaranteed amounts that can be used with a high degree of confidence in negotiating and closing a new-car purchase through the No-Enemies Buying Method.

CHAPTER VI

STEP #3: ARRANGING FINANCING

If a car buyer can pay cash for a new car, that's the best position to be in. A true cash buyer gains many advantages, as pointed out in Chapter III. The only time not to pay cash, in fact, would be if bank loans or financing plans carry interest rates low enough to make it worthwhile to keep money earning higher rates of interest.

Many consumers are going to need some kind of financing. Many consumers are also of the opinion that getting financing is a difficult and complicated task, one that only bankers and F&I managers truly understand. Most consumers, as a result, do not shop for their own financing, and wind up again at the mercy of the dealership sales system.

This is unnecessary, since any customer who walks into a new-car dealership with a pre-approved bank or credit-union loan becomes a one-pay cash buyer with as much control over the sales process as a true cash buyer.

Financing can be confusing, however, especially with the abundance of dealer advertising which includes financial claims and promises. The maze of dealer financing--rebates, incentives, low annual percentage rates (APR)--will be unravelled here. Other financial concerns, such as extended warrantees and other products, will be addressed in Step #6, Closing the Deal.

Right now, though, let's focus on what consumers can do about their financing situation before they get to the dealership.

The need for this focus is prompted by the explosion of long-term financing arrangements, no down-payment purchase plans, out-of-date and deceptive leases and other schemes that have brought some exorbitant profits on new-car deals to dealerships. That doesn't even consider the profits made on loans by banks, dealerships, leasing companies and other interest-earning institutions.

Many consumers have wound up owing thousands of dollars more than their new cars are worth, starting from the time they drive them out of dealer showrooms.

This situation is made possible whenever consumers make decisions about financing without understanding, or at least recognizing, the impact those decisions will have. Fortunately, this no longer has to be the case with the No-Enemies Buying Method.

There are three simple decisions a car buyer can make which minimize the financial impact of a new-car purchase on their lives and their pocketbooks. These are:

1. To pay off the full amount due on any outstanding loans on a trade-in, or at least try to attain a strong equity position;

Advantages and Disadvantages of Short Term Loans

For this example, assume an initial loan amount of $15,000, with the car depreciating to $8,000 in three years.

	36 Month Loan	60 month loan
Monthly Payment	$491	$326
Total Interest	$2,676	$4,560

Equity Position in Three Years

	36 Month Loan	60 Month Loan
Car Value	$8,000	$8,000
Net Payoff	-0-	7,256*
Net Equity	8,000	744

Disadvantages of Choosing 36 Months

A higher payment of $491 means there is $165 less monthly cash for three years.

Advantages of Choosing 36 Months

If you want to trade three years down the road, you will have $8,000 equity to put as down payment on a new car rather than only $744.

If you keep your car, you will save $7,824 in total payments for the next two years.

Conclusion: If you can manage the higher payment involved with a shorter loan term--24, 36 or 48 months instead of 60--your car's net value (equity) will be dramatically higher years down the road.

2. To make the highest cash down-payment on the new car that they possibly can;

3. To arrange as short a loan term as possible.

These ideas may be simple, but they are not necessarily easy. Yet making such tough decisions can produce some exciting surprises when coupled with the No-Enemies Buying Method.

If a customer pays thousands of dollars less for a new car, for example, he or she can often get the same monthly payment on a 36-month loan as a less-knowledgeable buyer would on a 60-month loan.

So, in three years instead of five, No-Enemies car buyers have a free-and-clear trade-in if they want to purchase a new car--not to mention all the interest they've saved on their shorter-term loan.

Making the tough decisions early, makes things easier in the long run. What it comes down to is this: Wouldn't it be nice to have a new car every three years that you can afford, while someone else who didn't make the tough decisions, is trapped for five years in the same car.

Remember, cars are not houses; they depreciate rapidly. When making the tough decisions about the length of a car loan to attain a comfortable monthly payment, realize that a car is a depreciating asset, losing value virtually every month. The shorter the loan term--36, 42, 48 months--the quicker the customer attains "equity," where the car is worth more wholesale than the amount owed.

Without keeping the car's equity position in check, minus equity problems arise (see below).

One of the biggest problems for new-car buyers is their lack of equity in their trade-in. The No-Enemies Buying

Method can help sort this out. The following steps should be closely followed whenever there exists an outstanding loan on a trade-in.

1. The buyer must call the lending institution holding the outstanding trade-in loan and ask for a "10-day net payoff" amount on the loan. That will give the buyer the amount of money required to release title to the trade-in if paid within 10 days. Net payoff is the sum that excludes any remaining interest left on the loan.

2. Determine if the net payoff can be reduced by cancellables, such as a service contract, life and disability insurance, or other "extras" financed on the old loan. (See the Buried Treasure feature at the end of this chapter.)

3. After finishing with the banks, determine the trade-in's value as described earlier. It will be either:

Minus-equity--the amount owed is greater than car's worth at wholesale, or

Plus-equity--car's wholesale value is greater than amount owed.

4. Continue on to the next step of the No-Enemies Buying Method, where these figures will be put to work.

A buyer with a positive equity value in his or her trade-in can use that value as all or part of the down payment on a new car.

Buyers with minus-equity trade-in values have five options at this point:

1. Pay down the old car loan as much as possible;

2. Increase the down payment on the new car, thus reducing the new-car loan required;

3. Retail the car in order to get the highest possible return, as described in Step 2, and forget about trading it in. Hopefully, this will allow repayment of the old car loan in full, and leave a little left over;

4. Include the money owed on the old car loan into the new-car loan. Obviously this will only work if your credit rating is sufficiently good that your lender will do it, and you choose to over finance;

5. Keep your car, and hold onto this book until your trade-in equity situation improves!

Whatever path the minus-equity car buyer chooses, none seem particularly attractive. Maybe that's why such a situation is referred to in the car industry as being "buried," "in the bucket," or "upside-down."

Remember, long-term loans, low down payments, dealer profits, depreciation and a continuing cycle of trading in cars without equity, all have contributed to buyers getting into such uncomfortable positions in the first place.

Once the tough decisions have been confronted, buyers are then ready to shop a few banks or credit unions for new-car loans that will meet their financial needs. As with shopping for used-car dealers earlier, consumers are likewise seeking only lender commitments, in this case known as a loan pre-approval.

First, call around to various banks requesting car loan information, including current interest rates, terms, and anything else that's available. There is a good chance that you will run into a friendly person or two, people you can call later on with questions that come up.

Remember that, just as dealerships sell cars at a markup, financial institutions are selling money at an interest rate. Both are looking to make a profit, which is their right and purpose.

Banks and credit unions are likewise part of the new era described in this book--an era where customer satisfaction rules the day. They are becoming quite assertive with their claims of meeting consumers' needs. Banks are doing things like cross-promoting car loans to savings account customers. Credit unions are boasting about their person- alized service, their intimate ties to the local economy, their member-run boards of directors, and their non-profit status.

So, look for banks and credit unions that offer the best deals and the highest commitment to customer satisfac- tion.

Buyers should also be looking for simple-interest loans. These are loans, in layman's terms, that will offer the lowest payoff amount should the loan be paid in full early.

Consumers should also be aware that some loans may contain any of the features listed below. Unless the total overall cost of loans containing these features is the lowest, try to avoid:

☐ Adjustable or variable interest rates.

☐ Loan fees ("points," origination fees, etc.)

☐ Rule of 78's loans. These loans are structured so that borrowers pay heavy interest early in the loan, and mostly principal toward the end--much like a home mortgage. Without getting into an accounting session here, when you pay a rule of 78's loan off early, for example in the first year it is opened, the balance due will be higher than if it had been a simple interest loan.

☐ Loans that have a prepayment penalty.

Since, by now, buyers should have a good idea of the amount of the loan they need, exact monthly payment quotes for the same amount and term --$15,000 over 48 months, for example--can be requested from each lender.

The aim of this exercise is to discover the lowest overall cost of a car loan, over its full term. The payment schedules should be carefully noted; if they are not the same from bank to bank, then the interest rates are different, or something else is going on.

Ask questions. Find out about origination or set-up fees, or points, as they are sometimes called. An origination fee on a loan with a low interest rate might be better over its full term than one with a higher rate and no initial fee.

There are other charges, however, that might be added into a payment quote, and these can cloud an accurate comparison between lenders. An excellent question to ask during this process is: "Are there any charges of any kind that are being applied to this loan?" Ignore, for the moment, such charges as those for credit life and/or disability insurance policies. Get only "bare" (no extras) payment schedules to allow accurate bank-to-bank comparisons.

The idea at this juncture is merely to get loan information from two or three different banks, credit unions or other lenders.

And, don't overlook the possibility of borrowing against a personal life-insurance policy or other low-interest vehicles such as home equity loans, which are becoming increasingly popular these days because their interest is usually tax deductible.

If consumers have done their homework, it will be very clear which lenders offer the best deals with no hidden charges or the lowest total cost. Just as importantly, which lenders sound like comfortable people to work with. If they are not willing or are hesitant to discuss their loan requirements and products freely over the phone, then they are likely not people that are interested in earning the customer's business.

Finally, when the sources have been narrowed down to one or a few over the phone, the next move is to visit them and confirm the information you have.

After completing these visits, it is then time to decide on the bank which seems best to do business with. Only then should the customer fill out a loan/credit application--and only with that single loan source--with the understanding that the final loan amount is not set yet, but that pre-approval, as mentioned earlier, will save time later on.

Many buyers already have a banking relationship, but they should shop other sources to ensure that their own lender is competitive.

This is also a good time to review the credit life/disability insurance policies offered by the lenders, if the buyer cares to purchase these options. The rates, terms, conditions and exclusions of these policies may vary substantially from bank to bank, and could be a factor in where you get your loan.

Whether insurance is a consideration or not, the lender is now in a position to finish up the loan paperwork for pre-approval. They can most often have a check ready the day, or day after they are called and told that negotiations with the car dealer are completed.

The final part of Step #3 is for consumers to become familiar with local dealerships' new-car newspaper ads, especially the fine print where they disclose the financing terms being offered. These few small words can tell consumers a lot about how the dealerships approach financing.

If one seems to have high interest rates, it is probably tacking on a percentage point or two to the rate it gets from the bank, and then rewriting a higher rate on the customer's loan contract, and pocketing the difference.

Call dealers and ask them which local lenders they work with. Then call the lenders, and ask them directly what interest rates they offer. You might be surprised at the difference. Effectively, what the bank will give you will be near the dealership's "buy rate" (the interest rate the bank charges them for new-car financing).

This is worth knowing, because the customer will be in a position later on to offer the sales manager the chance to sell dealer financing on the new-car deal. Sometimes, because of the high loan volume a dealership offers a bank, the dealership's buy rate will be lower than the bank's over-the-counter rate to its regular customers.

Factory rebates and low annual percentage rates (APRs) offered by manufacturers are another matter. There are a number of different types, but they all have two things in common: they are real money, and they are sponsored by the factory, not the dealer.

Unfortunately, consumers rarely differentiate factory programs from dealer promotions. Dealer promotions are in fact not real money, but usually discount gimmicks that are covered by an increased mark-up of the retail sticker price.

A $1,000 factory rebate, for example, is a check that the buyer can put in the bank.

A $1,000 "in-house dealer rebate," is only a discount, called "air" or "smoke" in the car industry, which describes its insubstantial nature. The dealer deducts that discount from the profit on the car sale, but the retail price was already marked-up to allow for the so-called discount.

Other such promotions are worked the same way. "Push, pull or drag your trade-in onto our lot and get $2,500," for example; or, "$2,000 discounts during our giant weekend blowout sale," and "6% interest available" are all examples of pure hype. Air. Smoke.

In the first two examples, if a dealer has $3,000 or more in markup, the dealer can pay for the promotion in full, and end up with lots of profit. In the last example, a bank will allow a dealer to "buy down" to any lower interest rate in return for partial, up-front cash.

Where does the dealer get the cash to buy down these interest rates? Out of a heavily marked-up sticker price, that's where. So are free microwaves, a trip to Bermuda, a free T.V. set--and those relatively inexpensive "freebies." All they mean is that a buyer is paying much more in the form of inflated sticker prices than the cost of the items themselves.

There are hundreds of examples. What buyers can do to protect themselves is to realize that if a deal sounds too good to be true, it probably is.

Factory-rebate and low-APR programs from manufacturers are true, however. The following steps should help
buyers find the real beef among the bologna:

☐ The simplest way would be to refer to a new-car pricing
printout, because this reveals what factory programs are
currently available.

☐ Read the fine print in newspaper advertising and watch
TV ads closely. (Automotive News, the industry newspaper
found at public libraries, has current listings of factory rebate
and incentive programs in each issue.) Look for the words
"manufacturer" and "factory," and beware of anything different. "Dealer cash incentives", also known as "factory-to-
dealer incentives", are particularly tricky. They actually do
come from the factory, but are only paid to dealers, not
buyers. As such, dealers can do what they want with the
money, including giving it to the buyer--which is one of the
goals of the No-Enemies Buying Method.

☐ Call dealership finance departments to find out what the
factory is offering in the way of rebates and low-interest rates
to the customer. Take notes, because these programs often
have fine print of their own.

There are many specialized factory rebates that are fairly
common but almost unknown, such as **first-time buyer**
and **college-graduate** rebates. If a customer qualifies for
these special rebates, they can be worth hundreds if not
thousands of dollars.

Domestic factories usually offer car buyers a choice
between a low APR and a cash rebate. The personal
financial realities of each buyer will to some degree govern
the decision between the two.

Most low-APR programs put conditions on the term of the loan at the low rate, usually making them short-term, 24- or 36-month payment schedules.

If a buyer, who needs a certain level of payment, can shop lenders for slightly longer-term loans, the best deal would be to take the cash rebate instead.

Consider the following scenario, where numbers are rounded to the nearest dollar, where the rebate is $1,000, and the APR is 7%:

In this example, taking the rebate means a saving of $360. And if a buyer intends to take the rebate and can afford to

	Taking the Rebate	Taking the APR
Amount to finance	**$9,000**	**$10,000**
APR	12%	7%
36 monthly payments	$299	$309
Total payments	$10,764	$11,124

pay off a loan early, there would be greater interest savings.

Again, an individual's financial situation will drive the choice between the two. However, there are a few rules which may be helpful in making that decision. Generally speaking, buyers might:

Take the cash rebate when...

☐ the amount of rebate exceeds or equals the amount of interest savings;
☐ the amount of the rebate is only slightly less than the amount of interest savings;
☐ buyers usually pay off their loans early;

☐   buyers tend to get only normal yields on savings;
☐   the high monthly payments of a short-term loan are too
high, even at the lower interest rate;

Take the special APR when...

☐   there are no rebates available and it is the best rate the
buyer can obtain;
☐   the amount of interest savings greatly exceeds the
amount of rebate;
☐   the payments will be made on or before their due date,
with no intention to pay off earlier;
☐   the buyer is a cash buyer for whom the cash that would
be used to buy the car could earn a higher yield than the
APR costs, if put into a savings or investment account
instead.

Thus, Step #3 of the No-Enemies Buying Method is designed to help consumers get their financing act together
long before meeting anyone at the dealerships. But that's
not all.

Consumers who have followed all of the first three steps
now have some very specific information about the car-
buying process--about choosing a car, about what its dealer
cost is, about how to handle a trade-in situation, about how
much cash down and which monthly payment amount is
optimum, and about rebates and APRs, to name a few.

Consumers also have probably gotten to know themselves a little better, and perhaps feel a little more comfortable with taking responsibility for their car-buying destiny.

No-Enemies car buyers can take all that knowledge and information, along with the pre-approved loan agreement, to the next step of the No-Enemies Buying Method.

And, they will take one other valuable thing along--increased confidence.

Is there buried treasure
in your old car loan?

Why is this area important?

☐ Because many American car owners owe money on their cars when they trade them in.

☐ If a customer has a loan balance of $5,000 outstanding on his trade-in, and $1,000 of this is cancellable, and if the customer does not use the cancellation process--or does not know about it--he or she is literally giving away $1,000.

☐ When calling their bank for the net balance owing (payoff) customers often accept that figure at face value, without realizing the balance might be greatly reduced.

☐ The amount that the balance can be reduced often means hundreds of dollars and sometimes more.

☐ Without knowing this, buyers can turn a great deal on a new car into an average deal. This is because they are grossly overpaying for the payoff of their old loan.

What is a "cancellable."

A "cancellable" is a dollar amount (premium) that was added on to the customer's car loan when the trade-in was originally purchased. These premiums would have been added to pay for extended warranties, credit life insurance, credit disability insurance, and in some cases, collision damage insurance.

Why are they called "cancellables"?

Because they can be cancelled, usually at any time, on a "prorated" or "unused portion" basis. "Any time" means it is solely the customer's discretion, whether the loan is paid off or not.

How does the customer know if the loan contains "cancellables"?

These premiums are disclosed on the customer's original loan contract. The customer should have a copy of this finance contract in the original car purchase paperwork. Also, the lender holding the loan has a copy that can be requested. Often, if lenders are cooperative, they can tell the customer immediately if any cancellables are contained in the original loan amount.

How does the customer go about cancelling these coverages?

Cancellation requests are normally made in writing and refunds are paid to the customer if the old loan is paid off. They will be applied against the existing loan balance if the loan is not actually paid off yet.

It is the customer's right and privilege to be refunded the unused portion of these coverages, but the cooperation of the institutions doing the refunding is often erratic for two major reasons.

1. Refunds are often considered a low priority administrative hassle.

2. Often a bookkeeping profit was recorded for the original sale of these premiums to the customers. As such, a loss must be taken by whatever department took the profit in the first place, once a cancellation occurs. These losses are known as "charge backs", and are feared by commission compensated or profit-loss responsible individuals, like the F&I manager, sales managers, general managers, lending institution branch managers, etc. Often, these people have their current month's paycheck reduced by these chargebacks to their departments.

The keys are persistence, following cancellation guidelines, and knowing your rights.

Wherever you purchased the coverages, be this the original selling dealership, the bank, etc., is where you go to cancel them. Often these institutions act only as agents representing an insurance company or "warranty company" that actually holds the policies or contracts. Cancellation procedures are normally written on these actual policies, which the customer should have a copy of. If the customer requests cancellation from, for example, the dealer, copies of the request should be mailed to those insurance and warranty companies just to make sure everyone is aware of what is happening. Often disputes arise as to when customers actually requested cancellation.

What happens if the customer's new-car purchase is "conditional" to receiving this refund, e.g., the $500 refund is needed for a down payment?

This can be a tricky area. Refunds cannot go directly to the customer until the old loan is paid off. At the same time, if the customer is buying a new car today, the old loan is still outstanding at the higher amount. There is no set answer for this timing problem, other than to involve all parties and bridge any communication gaps that might occur between the old dealer and old bank, and the new dealer.

If, during this process, it is not clear how much the re-fund is, who it is going to, exactly what will happen when it is received, or that everyone knows what is happening, then do not continue with your new-car purchase. Wait until the refund is actually applied against your old loan, creating an adjusted lower payoff.

Note: Dealers anxious for a new-car deal may often help the customer achieve quick refund results. Sometimes they will even credit the refund immediately and bear the burden of waiting for the actual refund from the other dealer, bank, etc.

To summarize, the area of receiving refunds from "cancellables" can be convenient and easy, if done prop-erly. Many institutions realize that it is not smart to put off the inevitable chargeback.

A final note is to people feeling they never purchased these insurances or "warranties". "Assumptive selling" is illegal yet quite common. Assumptive selling is when premi-ums are added to loans, and are only loosely disclosed or not disclosed at all to the customer. The only way to be cer-tain is to examine the original loan agreement.

If there is buried treasure, the customer must find it--no one else will.

CHAPTER VII

STEP #4: SEARCHING FOR DEALERS

Any good coach puts great emphasis on preparation before a contest, and the No-Enemies Buying Method is no different as it prepares buyers for new-car negotiations at the dealerships.

The emphasis on preparation is not to prepare buyers for a contest, but rather for no contest. The idea is to put an end to game playing.

So Step #4, not surprisingly, continues the preparation of consumers by attempting to increase their knowledge, confidence and sense of responsibility as car buyers.

The nucleus of the method is called **cost-plus buying**.

Simply defined, it means negotiating for a new car beginning with the dealer cost or invoice and working up to establish a purchase price rather than working down from the retail or sticker price.

Simply employed, cost-plus buying allows consumers to purchase the car they want at a price thousands of dollars less than ever before possible.

The unbelievable thing is that dealerships are ready, willing and able to work on this basis, even though they might realize a mark-up of only $200, rather than $2,000. Equally amazing, dealers who work this way will consider the car buyer a valuable friend during and long after the transaction is over.

The economic changes in the car industry, the ascendance of CSI, the high cost of holding slow-moving inventory, etc., are the major reasons why this is so. There are other, more specific reasons, such as the fact that dealers automatically get paid a so-called "hold-back" (usually 3 percent of dealer invoice) directly from domestic manufacturers and a few import car companies.

So, even selling a car at cost which carries a $10,000 invoice means the dealer still will make $300 at minimum, and there are other ways dealerships make money on car deals, as will be explained later on. But the building and maintenance of friendship is made possible for the customer only with the No-Enemies Buying Method.

The specifics of cost-plus buying will be detailed in Step #5; it is defined here so that the car buyer will know what to look for when searching for dealers.

In broad terms, cost-plus dealers are those with whom a buyer can negotiate a price for a new car that is near dealer invoice; that is, close to what the dealer paid for the car. A price can be negotiated by consumers on any model car sold in the United States (with the exception of those in short supply, and selected imports) that will come out somewhere between dealer invoice and $500 above invoice.

The first requirement, however, is to find the dealers who will work on a cost-plus basis.

If the car also carries a factory rebate of $1,000, then it is easy to see how the final price of the car could be well-below factory invoice. The newest trick in the book is for dealers to offer a car at a "net price" to the customer or "rebate already included" pricing. This means that the dealer keeps the rebate, not the customer. A "net price" of invoice, for a car that carries a $1,000 rebate, really means the customer is paying $1,000 over invoice.

Obviously, a No-Enemies buyer who pays dealer invoice would be keeping the rebate, thus paying **$1,000 below invoice.**

So it is back to the Yellow Pages and the phone once again. Consumers will want to contact sales managers at local dealerships, and might open conversation this way:

"I expect to be purchasing a new car within the next 48 hours, if you have what I want in stock, of course.

"I am a cash buyer with a trade-in which I've already bid wholesale, but you are welcome to bid on it as well. I am interested in buying such-and-such a model. What I'd like to know is how much over invoice you would accept, assuming it's a quick, clean deal."

This approach may seem unrealistic to skeptical readers, who may feel that this recommended up-front conversation with car people is impossible. However, it is suggested that these readers try the method, because it does work.

It is important to note here that sales managers and fleet managers are enamoured by clean deals. A clean deal is a

Negotiating
Do's and Don'ts

DO--Negotiate from invoice up, not sticker price down, and be informed (attain the dealer cost beforehand).

DO--Be positive and forthright, not belligerent or suspicious.

DO--Initially offer a little less than you will be willing to pay for the car.

DO--Initially ask for a little more than you actually expect to accept for your trade.

DO--Stay unemotional.

DO--Follow through with your promises.

DO--Stress the win/win No-Enemies philosophy and your belief in working together on customer satisfaction.

DO--Understand that even using a systematic buying method, buyers and sellers still like to negotiate!

*   *   *

DON'T--Start talking to dealers until you are a "cash" buyer--cash or pre-approved loan.

DON'T--Treat dealership personnel as anything but professional business people--unless they prove otherwise.

DON'T--Take anything personally--like trade value.

DON'T--Speak first. If asked what you'll pay or accept for a trade, put the ball in the dealer's court.

DON'T--Believe everything you're told. If you're told that a model is suddenly in great demand, look at the lot.

DON'T--Accept smooth answers to your questions about such matters as extra charges. Question everything.

DON'T--Be hesitant to end negotiations and leave.

DON'T--Work with a dealer or sales manager who is uncooperative.

DON'T--Be uninformed. Have your dealer invoice price and an idea of the wholesale trade value before negotiating.

DON'T--Be upset if the deal goes perfectly.

quick, no-nonsense transaction. This method teaches car buyers how to become a participant in a clean deal.

Back to the conversation: A negative response such as, "We don't work for nothing around here," indicates you've reached a sales manager that is either inexperienced or uninformed. There is no use in going further. In this case, one thing a shopper could say before parting company is "So, Mr. Sales Manager, if I offered you $5,000 over invoice, you wouldn't take it, right?" This approach will often break the ice with a chuckle, and allow business-like discussions to proceed.

Fortunately, most sales managers will welcome such an approach, and quickly get down to business. If the sales manager asks how much the customer is willing to pay over invoice, a confident answer is called for, such as "A whole-sale price as close to invoice as I can get."

Let the sales manager quote a markup first. You can always negotiate down from there. It is simply a case of supply and demand. Some models are hot, some are not. Some cars may be so limited in availability that no less than $2,000 over invoice would be considered.

On the other hand, a lot-full of last-year's models may be a strong inducement for a sales manager to sell a car at less than $200 over invoice, or even below invoice, just to move inventory. There are a lot of dealers, and the customer is doing the qualifying here, not the dealer. The idea is to find a starting point that the customer can accept from which a deal can be fairly negotiated later on.

Just what is a fair mark up? Only the market can tell. Once three sales managers have been contacted on an invoice-plus basis, the buyer should have a good idea of the local market and the desirability of the model being sought. If the markup does not seem favorable, out-of-town dealers should be shopped, and there should be some effort to work the markup down with the sales managers.

One of the most common myths about car buying today, is that one must return to the dealer where you bought the car for warranty repairs and scheduled maintenance. This is only folklore.

Customers can get maintenance and warranty work done at any chosen dealer, even if they bought their cars out of town.

Many factories spell out in their franchise agreements that warranty work can be done by any dealer bearing the factory name plate. Naturally, many dealers put their own customers first, so it might be useful to elevate your importance in the eyes of the service manager by finding an appropriate way to tell him that you are looking for a quality department that can do your work for years to come.

As described earlier, most service managers are entrepreneurs, running their department as a profit center. As such, you can expect red carpet treatment if you are seen as long term business--even if you bought your car from a direct competitor.

So, you are free to choose your dealer where you wish. The car buyer, at this point, uses the telephone and the No-Enemies Method to get all the prices involved (including sales tax figures and licence plate registration fees). This is when buyers will ask the sales manager for the dealer cost on the makes and models they are interested in, as well as any options desired. If a buyer has already taken advantage of a pricing service, this becomes an opportunity to compare figures.

A sales manager who quotes a figure well above the printout figure should be questioned about the difference. Again, writing it all down is a must. Confident, polite and professional questions will gain responses on just about anything from sales managers who want to do business.

After two or three such conversations with different sales managers, the customer should have a pretty good idea of the actual numbers a deal might involve. Let's put together a potential cost-plus new-car deal, by the numbers:

$ 15,000 Dealer invoice on desired model

+   **200** Mark-up agreed to by sales manager

+   **800** sales tax

+   **500** Registration and license plate fees

$ 16,500 Total

- **1,500** Cash down payment

- **1,000** Factory rebate to buyer

- **5,000** Actual Cash Value (A.C.V.) of trade-in

$ 9,000 "Out the door" amount to be financed

The above is the standard, simple method to use when calculating the amount to be financed to pay the dealership for a new car.

If a new-car buyer has an outstanding loan payoff on the trade-in, that payoff will increase the total amount that will have to be financed to complete the new-car deal, as in the following:

$ 9,000 "Out the door" financing required (see above)

+**$ 6,000** Payoff on trade-in loan

$ 15,000 Total amount of financing required.

It is imperative that the above means of calculation be followed to forever keep the numbers simple. It doesn't matter if the deal involves a minus-equity payoff--as was the case with the deal outlined in Step #3--or a plus-equity situation.

This is the only straightforward method of calculation that will remove the threat of potential financial complications or crafty dealer arithmetic that could wind up costing the buyer money.

Accept no substitutes!

Your use of the pricing service has made the strategy possible in black and white, while in the "old days" there was an element of blindness.

Getting back to the conversation, the buyer may hear the sales manager mention something about the availability of closeouts or demonstration models during the conversation. Switching customers to older or undesirable inventory is the first thing a good sales manager usually attempts when faced with a "wholesale buyer".

These models may be worth considering--but only if they are dramatically below dealer invoice or below the best deal on a brand-new model.

Although never titled to an individual, demos are cars that have been used, and closeouts are last year's models, and should be recognized as such. Demos are generally less attractive deals since factory warranties and other guarantees began the day the dealership put the demo into use. In most cases the buyer loses that portion.

A closeout might be a good deal if it carries a price thousands below invoice, and thus puts a desirable or financially unreachable model into a buyers price range. But closeouts are closeouts, usually because they were slow sellers or over-produced models. Later, when consumers try to sell cars bought as closeouts, they will usually find resale values to be low.

Deals for demos and closeouts call for caution, and require even closer scrutiny than new models.

As these issues are settled, the customer is in a position to calculate potential monthly payments:

☐ How long will the loan term have to be in order to get a comfortable monthly payment?

☐ What will the total interest be on the loan? Could or should more cash be put down to shorten the term or lower the monthly payments?

☐ Would it be wise to consider a less expensive model, even a closeout, or might a more expensive new car be within reach?

The thing to remember about all this is that negotiations haven't even begun yet. No final decisions have been made yet; adjustments can still be made. Nor is there a need for consumers to be rushing all over town from dealership to dealership, trying to get a better price or find the model desired. All of this is happening over the phone! Any adjustments the buyer has to make in financing, options or model desired can be quickly and easily made from the comfort of home or office.

Not a bad way to shop for a car!

All that's left of Step #4 is a phone call to the sales manager of the dealership that looks the best for an appointment and a test drive.

CHAPTER VIII

STEP #5: DRIVING AND DEALING

When ready to commit to a deal, it's off the phone and onto the lot. If buyers are clear in their own minds that they are committed cost-plus buyers, then they are ready, willing and able to deal.

As soon as a customer shows up on the dealership lot to test drive a car and meet the sales manager in person, a metamorphosis takes place. The customer becomes a committed cost-plus buyer, and a customer, all at once.

All the shopping is over, the phone work finished. Consumers have to this point represented themselves as cash or pre-approved loan buyers who plan to buy a particular car within 48 hours (or some short, specific time frame), as long as everything discussed on the phone is as represented.

All that's left, in the sales manager's mind, is to negotiate the details of the cost-plus deal that was presented on the phone.

If buyers have any reservations at this point about going through with the deal, then they should get back to the phone and cancel the appointment.

Before arriving, the customer's insurance agent and the financial source that holds the loan pre-approval should have been alerted to the meeting, so they can move ahead with their paperwork as soon as the deal is made.

Upon arriving, there is no time or reason to browse the showroom--besides, sales people are there, prowling for an "up." Head directly to the sales manager's office to keep the appointment.

And when introduced to the sales manager, make certain it is indeed the sales manager, and not just a senior sales-man or sales team leader. Simple diplomacy by consum-ers--or a look at the organization chart hanging in most dealership showrooms--will satisfy them concerning the person's name and title. And immediately requesting a business card is also prudent.

Polite ground rules should be set immediately, by the customer, when he or she meets the sales manager. If the desire is to test drive a car and sleep on the decision to buy overnight, let the sales manager know that a buying deci-sion will be made within 24 hours, or by the next day.

Commitment, in other words, does not mean throwing caution to the wind. At the same time, setting ground rules should not mean being overbearing.

Likewise, there should be no hesitation on the part of customers, just as was true on the phone, to cut off any conversation if the dealership sales system seems to be kicking into action, or the greeting is anything less than courteous.

If a sales person is assigned to help a customer with the test drive, by the way, that doesn't mean a buyer is about to be victimized. It is more likely that the sales manager has decided to reward the salesman by letting him work with the cost-plus buyer. The salesman will get a flat commission and, since profit is not a factor, all the buyer gets is service. It is the sales manager's prerogative to do this; make certain, however, that the sales manager will be available after the test drive.

Now is not the time for negotiations, anyway; now is the time for customers to touch, look at and listen to the new car they have come to test drive.

If you think you are going to negotiate for that car, jot down the VIN (or vehicle identification number), usually located on a small metal tag inconspicuously riveted to the driver's side front-door jamb. That can be compared later on to the VIN number of the sales manager's invoice, to avoid miscommunication.

Since the buyer is prepared to buy the car if all is as advertised, it should be gone over with a fine-tooth comb. If some less-than-crucial option is not included, or if the color is wrong, such things can usually be straightened out easily by the sales manager.

But on the other hand, if the car does not measure up to the requirements stated earlier over the phone, continue to shop.

Needless to say, cost-plus buyers know enough not to get trapped by a sales pitch for another model. It is still the customer's choice. If there is another model to see at that dealership, move to that one; otherwise, leave the dealership.

The sales manager may have instructed the sales person to go over the details of the deal, after the test drive. Consumers need not have a problem with this, as long as they remain aware of the pitfalls of the dealership sales system. If any games are played, ask to see the sales manager, or leave the lot immediately.

If consumers have done proper phone preparation, sales managers already know they are dealing with a cost-plus buyer. If a specific cost-plus deal was not established over the phone--say, $200 over dealer invoice--now is the time to do so.

Now is also the time to really show off the qualities of a No-Enemies car buyer, without acting superior or aggressive, naturally. Consumers would do well to pepper the conversation with calm, simple and polite statements of fact that highlight their knowledge, particularly about CSI (see Chapter III), and the intention to follow through with a glowing response to factory questionnaires--without threatening the dealership with a bad one if the deal doesn't go well! Blackmail is not recommended in this method, and neither is a hard sell, by the dealer--or the consumer!

Such good attitudes will have a very positive effect on sales managers, and will beat, hands-down, any power-driven argument to gain the upper hand in a car-buying situation.

Now a word about trade-ins. If trading in the car at the dealership is not advantageous, consumers must be certain they can dispose of it before they sign the deal for a new one.

If the dealership takes trade-ins, consumers should remember that there may be an advantage to this course of action, even though they already have a wholesale bid or even a retail buyer in the wings. The advantage is that, in most states, sales tax is only paid on the difference between the price of the new car and the trade-in allowance.

If the sales manager proffers an appraisal that is equal or close to the wholesale bid, giving the trade-in to the dealership is a plus. A $3,000 trade-in allowance that can be fully applied to the price of a new car would save the customer $240 on sales tax, figured at 8%. (See Chapter V for a review of trade-in considerations.)

Obviously, things like sales tax and luxury tax will be much more significant in this decision making process when expensive new cars and high value trade-ins are involved.

Another decision is involved if the dealer has added any options, either actually installed or not yet installed, they will appear on the "second sticker", and it will have been the dealer's conscious decision to place them there. Such options are an important red flag. The mark-up on these items might be anywhere from two to five times their cost. A buyer has every right to negotiate the price of these options, or simply to refuse them.

Remember, a cost-plus buyer, in establishing a $200-above-invoice selling price, for example, has set that figure for the entire deal, including the options.

Question everything, assume nothing, and don't blindly accept anything. Go over the entire transaction with the sales manager on paper--including the invoice dollar amount, rebates, options, registration fees and sales tax, with or without the trade-in allowance--making sure that the bottom-line "out-the-door" price is clearly understood.

Always insist on seeing the actual invoice. A credible sales manager will have no problem with this request.

Eyes and ears should be open for any hidden charges, especially pure mark-up charges like "additional documentation fees" and "dealer prep," or pass-through charges such as "advertising fees," which are normally prepaid by the manufacturer. Even check the VIN number of the car on the sales manager's invoice against the one copied down earlier during the test drive.

Consumers can be comfortable during this process, and should strive to make sales managers feel the same way about them. After all, the sales manager has already agreed to a mark-up over the phone, with someone who sounded like a knowledgeable customer. So well-educated, in fact, that nearly the entire deal was laid out with a single phone call.

Now that the sales manager has met the customer in person, it should be obvious that he or she is, indeed, as advertised, a confident individual with a good understanding of the car-buying process. Not only that, the customer is acting responsibly, interested in helping the dealer with a good report to the factory, with referrals and by becoming a repeat customer, who will also be using the dealership's service and parts departments.

Not a bad way to sell a car!

The No-Enemies Buying Method by now may look as good to the sales manager as it does to the cost-plus buyer.

CHAPTER IX

STEP #6: CLOSING THE DEAL

The last stop before closing the deal on a new-car purchase may be the finance & insurance office.

Dealerships usually designate the F&I manager to write sales contracts, rather than the sales manager. This keeps the sales manager selling instead of writing contracts.

It also allows the F&I manager, who is specifically trained in the dealership sales system, to sell "back-end" products, financial and otherwise. Unsuspecting buyers could find this visit lengthy and expensive, particularly those without any buying plan. That leaves them open to make on-the-spot buying decisions, without really understanding what they've agreed to.

No-Enemies Buyers, on the other hand, have been aware of and preparing for this meeting from the beginning, for here is where the climax of the car-buying process occurs: The signing of the sales contract.

It is imperative that a sales contract, exactly stating the numbers and terms agreed to with the sales manager, is prepared before any other conversation takes

place between the buyer and the F&I manager or whomever does the paperwork.

It is simply good business practice to get a deal on paper before taking it any further. Several things happen when the sales contract is prepared and on the table:

1. The buyer can see and dispute any variances, or simply ask questions, before getting into closing the deal;

2. The bottom-line or "out-the-door" figure on the contract, which is also the amount to be financed, is clearly defined--preventing a F&I manager from "automatically" adding anything on;

3. The mere fact that the contract was asked for tells a good F&I manager that the buyer is educated and worthy of being treated as such.

Once the initial paperwork is complete, the buyer must continue in control of the negotiating process with the F&I manager. As in earlier parts of the negotiations, that is accomplished by immediately establishing ground rules. Deliver some version of the following statement to the F&I manager:

"I have been pre-approved for a loan at such-and-such a bank or credit union, which I intend to use to pay the balance due on this contract within 24 hours, at which time I will take delivery on the car.

"I understand there are some products that you will be presenting to me now, but I have to tell you that I will not be making any buying decisions about them today. However, I will take any brochures or other information you may have to offer concerning them.

"I also understand that you offer your own financing at this dealership. I don't necessarily expect you to offer me your 'buy rate,' but what would be your best interest rate on a 48-month loan in the amount stated on the contract?"

Listen carefully to the F&I manager, and take careful notes. It is possible that a lower interest rate might make dealer financing desirable. If buyers intend to take advantage of that, they should be doubly careful with the amount to be financed.

This amount should stay the same as the one worked out with the sales manager, and the numbers for the interest rate, term and total interest should wind up the same on the loan agreement as the ones presented by the F&I manager.

No-Enemies buyers have already done their homework on financing, so the numbers and terms should be very clear. The sales manager's presence can be requested at any time to insure that there is no misunderstanding about terms and conditions with the F&I manager--who might try to convince the buyer of a whole new set of terms and conditions.

Careful, though; this is a place where finance managers are very prone to "slip in" extra charges, like credit life or disability insurance. This is the time to choose the insurance coverages reviewed earlier in Step #3.

Again, buyers should agree to no extras of any kind that they have not thoroughly reviewed and understood in terms of their nature and price. What the buyer should be looking to attain in the finance office includes these specific goals:

1. To leave the dealership that day with the same unpaid balance (out-the-door balance) that was worked out and agreed to by the sales manager and written down on the contract;

2. To remain cool and collected in the face of an aggressive sales presentation of back-end products by the F&I manager;

3. To discover if dealer financing can save money over that already arranged;

4. To complete and sign the contract and any forms necessary to finalize the deal.

And that's all. No matter what, it is important for buyers to remember in the F&I manager's office that they can leave the dealership if they feel they are being lied to or mistreated in any way.

If things even hint at deviating from the contract already worked out, remember the sales manager is in the wings, ready to help you. There are few sales managers who will jeopardize a deal because a buyer is not giving in to sales pressure from an F&I manager.

Above all, buyers should try to make their stay in the F&I office a brief one, and give total and undivided attention to what the F&I manager has to say. No matter what pressure or tactics are applied by the F&I manager to add anything to the contract, the simple answer is a firm, "No, thank you."

What buyers must realize is how highly trained and experienced a good F&I person is. As described in Chapter 2, the F&I office is a significant profit center for the dealership. Extended warranties might cost the dealership $300 and be sold for $1,000; undercoating and chemical packages might cost the dealership $100 and be sold for $500; 40% of life and disability premiums go straight into the dealership bank account.

It is your choice to take or reject these products, and their quality, price and profit will vary. But, anything from undercoating to an extended protection plan can be shopped and purchased days or weeks after your transaction, and on a cost-plus basis.

The signing of the contract only happens after the buyer is satisfied with the deal, and even then the buyer still has an option: in most states, even though the contract is signed, a car deal is not legally done until the buyer accepts delivery of the new car.

F&I Products

Extended Warranties--more correctly known as service contracts, mechanical breakdown insurance, etc. Unlike what many consumer advocates imply, they are not alike. There is a huge variety, some backed by insurance companies, some by manufacturers, some dealer "in-house" programs.

These service contracts cover selected components that are not covered by the manufacturers' warranty. Most pay manufacturer deductibles and have fringe benefits like towing, rental car reimbursement, etc. Some new plans pay for maintenance, even wear. Some plans are superb, others almost worthless. Shop for service contracts only after you buy your car, and then on a cost-plus basis. Shop at least three or four dealers.

Be sure to read the actual contract, not just the brochure. And, query service managers about how they handle claims, especially about what they cover and don't cover, and about the speed and convenience of claims.

Also, understand that no two policies are completely alike in coverage or price--they all sound good, but few are.

Credit Life & Disability--Decreasing term insurance can be added to your loan agreement. This type of insurance will pay off your loan in case of death, or make your payments if you become disabled. These are generally very expensive coverages, but usually have no qualifiers.

The policies differ as do the premiums, so shop around, checking for exclusions, waiting periods, etc. Read the actual policy, for the insurance offered may affect where you choose to get a loan.

The decision to buy insurance should be based on your current insurance portfolio, age, and health risk category.

Chemicals--This includes undercoating, paint, sealant, fabric protector, rust proofing, etc.

All new cars have some type of corrosion warranty from the factory, but usually for rust-through only. Read the fine print on the contract and warranty.

The "chemical" area of aftermarket products is very controversial. The question is actual value, regardless of cost. Consider not buying chemicals unless you have a strong feeling about their value or unless they can be purchased on a cost-plus basis.

Shop around, including specialty shops; don't limit your shopping to dealerships, because companies such as Ziebart usually offer superior products.

CHAPTER X

TAKING DELIVERY & FOLLOWING UP

Taking delivery of a new car is the crowning moment of the car-buying experience. It can be a very satisfying moment, especially if the car also represents thousands of dollars saved through cost-plus buying.

But buyers should wait until they get the car home to celebrate. Before the promised delivery date, buyers should be reviewing the contract, going over the financing arrangements and mentally double-checking everything about the deal. Then, when the date arrives, the only thing left to do is to actually take delivery.

The buyer's responsibility now is to make sure the deal is completely satisfactory and the car is absolutely perfect. All services should be properly performed, and all standard and optional equipment should be in place and operational. The car should be spotless, inside and out, with no flaws in finishes or upholstery.

All options and features should be explained, including the owner's manual, maintenance schedule, service record and the factory warranty book. An extra set of keys should also be provided.

If anything--anything at all--is missing or needs to be done on the vehicle, get it in writing, and think twice about taking delivery until it is corrected. Even a little fix often becomes a low priority to the dealership once the car leaves the lot.

Also, the dealership knows that the car deal is not legally binding until the buyer actually takes delivery of the car. In most states, the commonly invoked 72-hour "cooling off" period, which gives buyers three days to rescind a retail contract, does not apply when a customer has taken delivery of an automobile from the dealer's place of business. The sales manager, the service manager and everyone else connected with the deal will therefore be anxious to make delivery happen as soon as possible.

Buyers only have to make certain that delivery is accepted on their own terms. No matter what inducements are offered concerning taking delivery, buyers should remember that they are the ones who will be living with the car and the deal for a long time, not with the inducements.

It is very likely that a car dealership will want to be very accommodating--particularly since the factory is pressuring it to be that way. In fact, anyone who hasn't bought a car in the last few years might be surprised at the distance that some car dealers today are willing to go, as a matter of course.

The No-Enemies Buying Method will have paid off in any event, not only with a great price, but a great car as well.

Now is the time for some serious celebration, and maybe a little gratitude. It doesn't take much to say thank you to the people who worked on the deal before leaving the dealership.

It takes hardly any effort at all to write a thank-you letter to the sales manager for the way he or she handled the deal. A letter to the owner of the dealership, mentioning all the people who helped make the deal possible, wouldn't hurt, either. No mention need be made of the financial arrangements in the letter--unless, of course, buyers want their private financial dealings posted on the dealership's bulletin board. That's exactly where these letters will wind up, too, since they go a long way in building the esprit de corps of dealership organizations--most of which are under consumer attack.

These informal and formal thank-you notes will be remembered, and will help insure the red-carpet treatment the next time the No-Enemies buyer enters that dealership.

There are further followups the buyer should under take, and most of them require hardly any effort. Making those promised referrals of other buyers to the dealership is one--those buyers having read this book, of course. If a cost-plus buyer got a hassle-free deal, saved a bundle of money and got a great car from a dealership, it makes sense to buy his or her next car from the same place, doesn't it?

Undoubtedly, the most important thing a cost-plus customer can do for good dealerships is really simple: Give them the high marks they deserve on those customer satisfaction questionnaires from the factory. A "perfect 10" will bring up a dealer's CSI rating, and they know it.

It is a good idea for the buyer to let the dealership know that they have not forgotten about it, either. Buyers could send off a note to let the sales manager know about that great score they just gave the dealership. If the buyer's answers would be negative, the dealership wants to hear that too. Buyers so seldom call the dealer before blasting them on these forms that the dealer will remember the one who did.

There is absolutely no question that dealerships in the 1990s would sooner correct a problem than get a bad customer satisfaction rating.

If a buyer is not satisfied with treatment received from the dealership after the sale in any area, and no satisfaction is gained by talking to the dealer, a call to the area factory representative should get some action.

For any form of customer complaint, most car companies have a local zone office, and even an 800-number factory hotline. (These matters are discussed in more depth in the appendix, How to Resolve an Automotive Dispute.) These sources will usually get the dealership off the dime.

That last suggestion completes the No-Enemies Buying Method. It may seem paradoxical that a method which promotes peace and friendship between car buyers and dealers should end on a note of contention.

Unfortunately there is little if anything that is quite perfect in the world.

Car buying should become easier, however, when there are fewer enemies.

The Step by Step Route
to No-Enemies Car Buying.

STEP 1---GATHERING INFORMATION

- ☐ Obtain dealer cost information
- ☐ Evaluate needs
- ☐ Read consumer magazines, and obtain brochures
- ☐ Talk to friends, neighbors
- ☐ Note makes/models you like
- ☐ Visit car lots after closing
- ☐ Rent a car you like for a day
- ☐ Define exact car and options desired

STEP 2--- EVALUATING A TRADE-IN

- ☐ Consult used-car price books and services
- ☐ Improve look of car
- ☐ Get bids from dealers and try to sell privately
- ☐ Determine trade-in's actual cash value
- ☐ Obtain loan payoff, if necessary

STEP 3--- ARRANGING FINANCING

- ☐ Investigate banks and credit unions
- ☐ Determine cash down payment
- ☐ Figure maximum monthly payments
- ☐ Investigate dealer financing
- ☐ Find out about factory rebate, dealer incentives
- ☐ Obtain a pre-approved car loan

STEP 4-- SEARCHING FOR DEALERS

- [ ] Telephone several sales managers and take notes
- [ ] Present invoice-plus/CSI plan
- [ ] Get total cost from one dealer
- [ ] Review financing requirements

STEP 5-- DRIVING AND DEALING

- [ ] Meet sales manager of choice
- [ ] Confirm earlier discussions
- [ ] Test drive car and write down VIN
- [ ] Negotiate invoice-plus deal
- [ ] Keep all rebates/incentive; accept no extra charges
- [ ] Get contract showing all costs
- [ ] Figure amount to be financed

STEP 6---CLOSING THE DEAL

- [ ] Set ground rules for F&I manager
- [ ] Call in sales manager if needed
- [ ] Buy no warranties, etc., on spot
- [ ] Review dealer financing
- [ ] Sign only the contract containing terms you negotiated with the sales manager

STEP 7--DELIVERY & FOLLOWING UP

- [ ] Take delivery only if:
- [ ] All negotiations are completed
- [ ] Car delivered is as agreed
- [ ] If all's well after delivery:
- [ ] Write thank-yous and respond to questionaires
- [ ] Recommend dealer to others
- [ ] Buy next car from same dealer

Chapter XI

THE OTHER CHOICE

Choice.

The No-Enemies Buying Method is all about choice. As this method evolved, I concluded there are two intelligent ways to buy a car; in effect, two choices.

Customers can use this book--or some other credible how-to buying strategy--coupled with accurate dealer cost information, or they can seek the services of a professional who will do it for them.

Here in the real world, actually negotiating a new-car purchase themselves may not be the choice for many car buyers, for any number of good reasons.

People can, in most areas of their lives, choose to hire a professional to act on their behalf, such as CPAs or attorneys who would prepare taxes or write wills. However, such an option has not been available to the car-buying public. Until now.

Now, my company, U.S. Car Buying Service, can be enlisted to actually negotiate new-car deals on your behalf, using the No-Enemies Buying Method. For many it will be the best and simplest way to buy a new car at the lowest possible price.

Once you have read this book, I encourage you to call toll free at 1-800-CAR-TIME, at no cost or obligation. One of my staff members will explain the service, how it works, and answer any questions you might have.

If you elect the service, we will help you determine exactly what you want in a new car, from color to wheel covers. Our 25 years of auto expertise, coupled with a high-tech dealer cost database, will help sort out models, options and equipment packages.

"Models" doesn't sound like a complicated area, but in the 1991 model year, a Toyota pickup buyer had 27 models to choose from. Honda Accord shoppers had 17 choices.

Then, we will use the selected model's dealer cost figure, and establish an agreeable wholesale markup as a target for us to shoot for. No further steps will be taken until you give us the go-ahead.

By doing it this way, not only can you enjoy car shopping from the comfort of home or office, but you also are not apt to make any costly emotional decisions during the process. Simply stated, you cannot be subject to the profit-oriented dealership selling system if you aren't at the dealership making buying decisions.

Once a vehicle and target price has been established, we will then contact dealers in your local area, including any you might prefer to work with. Some of our clients have emphatically requested we not contact a certain dealer due to a bad experience in the past. We have this flexibility because we are able to shop any of the 24,000 plus dealers in the country.

Because we work in your best interests, if we find any savings during the process, those savings are passed on to you, the buyer. Also, we have specific guidelines dealers must follow that ensure you won't be subject to tricks, gimmicks, extra charges or hassles from the dealership when you actually take delivery.

When the exact car you want has been found and a deal arranged, all you have to do is show up at the dealership, sign the papers, and drive home in your new car. It is not unusual for this process to take only 15 or 20 minutes.

The only cost for this service, regardless of the time involved, is a flat fee of $250, with a 100% satisfaction guarantee. If you are not completely satisfied with the deal or the experience, there is no charge.

What comforts many buyers is our toll free hotline. At any time during the process, especially when taking delivery of the new car, our customers can call us 24 hours a day if there are any difficulties or any questions or concerns.

With factory rebates being so predominant today, many of our clients pay a price that is below dealer cost. It is easy to see how this benefits our clients, but we are often asked why dealers will work this way--selling cars for next to nothing.

Financially, dealers can usually justify selling a car wholesale if the deal can be made quickly and cleanly, as described earlier in this book. They will also be swayed to go the extra mile on both the price and customer satisfaction if they believe they will obtain volume in return, not to mention CSI ratings if a happy customer returns a glowing questionnaire to the factory in 30 days.

In fact, wholesale deals are a way of life with dealers. Most have designated fleet departments with managers who's sole task is to generate high volume on a monthly basis--at "corporation client" wholesale prices, of course. The problem for the average consumer is the fleet department is usually not accessible.

U.S. Car Buying Service helps customers gain access to the wholesale world within a car dealership--as does the No-Enemies Buying Method. Our customers are not presented to a dealership until they are ready to buy. In fact, if customers are in a shopping mode, or information gathering mode as described in Chapter III, they are encouraged by us to continue the process before we go to bat for them at a dealership. Our Shopping Package is designed specifically for that purpose. For $50, shopping customers obtain a copy of this book, two free dealer cost printouts, 30 days access to our Dealer Cost Hotline, where up to ten different makes can be quoted over the phone as to what their cost is, and, finally, a coupon entitling them to a discount of $50 on the buying fee if they choose to have us do it for them. The same number, 1-800-CAR-TIME, is used to order this service.

Whichever choice you make, car shopping--once a tortuous experience--can now be a fun, easy, money saving process with No-Enemies along the way....

Only friends.

Car Buyers' Math

The only formulas a car-buyer needs
to calculate a cost-plus new-car deal

Example	Formula Elements	Your Deal
+$15,000	Dealer invoice on the car you want	_____
+$200	Mark up agreed to by the sales mgr	_____
+$800	Sales tax	_____
+$500	Registration/Plates	_____
=16,500	**Total**	_____

Calculating the total fiancing required

-$1,500	Cash downpayment	_____
-$1,000	Factory rebate to buyer	_____
-$5,000	Actual cash value of trade-in	_____
=$9,000	Amount to be financed	_____
+6,000	Payoff off of loan on Trade-in	_____
=$15,000	Total financing required	_____

How to Resolve an Automotive Dispute

For those car or truck owners who have on-going problems with their vehicles; for those who are experiencing communication difficulties with the dealer or manufacturer; for those who have concerns about recalls or other factory questions, all manufacturers have channels of communication set up for the benefit of consumers.

The National Automobile Dealers Association has a 33-page directory that lists each factory dispute resolution program, including detailed information of how to contact each manufacturer.

The directory lists national and regional zone offices, has many toll free hotline numbers, and is otherwise a valuable tool for consumers.

The directory is available free of charge from Greg Meakin's business office. Consumers need only call the number listed below, or write to obtain a free copy.

If there is urgent information needed immediately, the representative answering the call will be happy to provide the consumer any applicable details over the phone, on the spot.

Greg Meakin
509-A N. Tamiami Trail
Venice, FL 34292
Phone (813) 485-8500

Consumers may also receive information, including the directory listed above, by contacting:
National Automobile Dealers Association
Consumer Affairs Department
8400 Westpark Dr.
McLean, VA 22101
Phone (703) 821-7144

Car Sales Lingo Dictionary

Sales Office Terms

Tight/Snuggy/Mooch---Tough bottom line buyers, who often sacrifice quality for low price.

Payment Mooch---Payment buyer.

Spot'em/Roll'em---Deliver the car to the customer on the spot (before the customer changes his mind!). A spot dealership is one who does this on most deals.

Two pounder---$2,000 in profit.

Quarter deal---$2,500 in profit.

Mini---The minimum flat commission payable.

Spiff---Extra bonuses.

Buck---$100; buck and a quarter is $125; buck and a half is $150; and buck six bits is $175.

Gross---Profit. "How much gross are you holding?" means the same as "How much profit is there in the deal?"

Hard Adds---Optional equipment that is not factory installed, such as audio equipment, sun roof, air conditioning, etc.

Soft Adds--An optional item not included in the manufacturer's list of options. Generally this is a protection package or extended warranty.

Low Ball---Quoting the customer less than the trade-in is really worth wholesale. Used to adjust a customer's expectations.

Gut Shoot---A verb that describes a dealer selling a vehicle at a give-away price. A sales manager advertising many give-away prices might declare to his sales force, "I'm gut shooting leaders all over the lot."

Screamer/Bubble---Creating a fantasy price, payment, or type of car, which is usually impossible to attain. The technique is used with a customer who is going to continue to shop.

They come back, and then the sales person bursts the bubble. Used in the following context: "I put him out on a bubble"; "I bubbled him"; or "I put him out on a screamer."

Line Price---The price the sales person verbally quotes, usually on used cars. Ideally, customers are "lined" as high as possible.

Low Line---The sales person makes the mistake of pricing the car too low. Sales people who "low line" too much will not be employed long.

Wood ya take/Mooch him on---Gradual decreases in price to attain commitment from the customer.

If I could . . . , would ya?---The most common commitment line. Remember the salesman said "if". "If I could get this car to you for $5,000 instead of $7,000, would you take it today?"

Loss leader --- A car advertised at a very low price to lure customers on the dealer's lot.

Switch Car---A nice, more expensive model, to switch people to if they don't like a loss leader.

Turn/Turnover/TO---Give the customer to a different salesman.

Blow him out/Walk him---Let the customer leave the dealership.

He's for real/He's on---Customer is committed to buy today.

First Round/Hit Him Between the Eyes---The initial deal presented to the customer in actual negotiations. These are usually very negotiable numbers.

Scrape him off the ceiling--Give him the second deal after the customer gets mad at the first round.

Grinder---A sales person who can "grind it out" with the customer, negotiating for hours without getting fed up. Also can describe a customer.

An up---A customer who walks onto the lot or into the showroom. "Who's up" is a sales person asking another sales person whose turn it is to take this "up."

Split---When two sales people work together to sell a car they usually split the commission.

Take a run---Meet the customer and try to sell him immediately.

Closer---The last person in sales to finish the deal. Usually a sales manager, but could be a salesman as well.

House---The dealership. Also called the "store".

The Desk---The sales manager's desk where deals are submitted by the sales force. Used as a verb or a noun, e.g., "to desk a deal," or "What does the desk say about the deal?" Sales manager is known as a desk man.

R.O.s---Repair orders for the service department.

Happy Tag/Temp Tag---Customer's temporary paper license.

Dealer Tag---A special license plate that is assigned to the dealer, not to a specific vehicle.

Write Up---The initial commitment made by a customer. It is brought to management by a salesman.

After Market---Optional equipment, not factory installed, that is sold or installed by the dealer or outside installer.

App---An abbreviation for application. "You'll need to fill out a credit app."

Locate--To find a vehicle for dealer exchange with another dealer.

Monroney/Sticker/First Sticker/MSRP --- The "manufacturer's suggested retail price." Monroney was the Congressman who initiated the legislation to have the MSRP posted on cars.

Old Car Price---A vehicle still on the dealer's lot that was delivered to the dealer before a price increase. Once on the car, the MSRP cannot be changed to a higher price.

On the Ground---A vehicle at the dealership.

Spot---To let the customer take possession of the vehicle "on the spot" before full payment is made or loan approval is given.

Tag(s)---License plate(s). Often described as "tax and tags," or "T&L" (tax and license fees).

Cars

Gutslick/Good eyeball/Cherry/Berry/Puff---The car looks good and is a desirable model.

Edgy/Dog/Rat/Slider/Sled/Raggedy---The trade is in bad condition.

Miler---Has high mileage.

A heavy---A large luxury car like a Cadillac or Lincoln.

Rig---Truck or R.V.

Dooley---Truck with dual rear wheels.

Ice Cold Air---The air conditioning works.

Hole in the roof---Sunroof.

First figure---Low, wholesale book value.

Guts---The interior, e.g., vinyl guts, leather guts.

Strippy---Very little equipment.

Tranny--Transmission

ACV---The actual cash value (wholesale) as determined by an appraiser for a trade-in.

U/A---Underallowance. The customer has received less than ACV.

O/A---The customer has received more than ACV, or an over allowance.

Smoke Car---A car bought at well below book value. Since banks use book to determine how much can be loaned, the difference, or "smoke", can be structured by the dealer as a down payment that really isn't. This helps with low down, no down or minus-equity buyers.

Clock---The odometer.

Bambi Beige--A tan car, usually less desirable for resale.

Finance Office Terms

Strokes---Monthly payments.

Baby Strokes---Low monthly payments.

Buried/Upside down/In the bucket---The outstanding loan on the trade is much greater than the value of the car.

Downstroke---Cash down payment.

Croak and choke/LAHA---A description for Life, Accident and Health insurance.

Penny Roll---Also known as high penny roll, it means rolling monthly payments up to the nearest 99 cents. Thus, a $250 a month loan becomes $250.99, an increase customers rarely object to but which is $59.40 in dealership profit over the life of a 60 month loan. An aggressive version is rolling a payment of, say, $271.00 to $279.99. Over $500 more profit would be earned in this example.

3-Way/Chemmies/Snake oil---Chemical packages including rust proofing, under coating, paint sealant, fabric and vinyl protector.

Bucket/Chute/Box--The finance office itself, e.g., "the customers are in the chute," or "in the box."

Packed payment/Loaded payment---Quoting the customer a payment that includes extended warranties, credit insurance, etc. The actual premiums are only disclosed after most things are signed.

Cut a reader---Wrote a check.

Cut a hot reader---Wrote a check that bounced.

How Much Up---How much over invoice, e.g., "It will take six-up to buy that car" means $600 over invoice is an acceptable deal.

Hard money/Real money---Actual cash down payment, or ACV on a trade. No rebates, air, smoke or allowances are included.

Hold Check---A deferred down payment. The hold check enables the dealer to make the sale and the customer can take immediate delivery.

Buyer's Order---The sales contract for the purchase of the vehicle. Also called a sales order, purchase order, or vehicle purchase agreement.

Nickel deal---$500 in profit on the deal.

"G" deal/Dime deal---$1,000 in profit on the deal.

Dozen deal---$1,200 in profit.

Get'em bought--Get the customer approved for his car loan. "Is he bought?" means is the customer approved yet.

Mickey the down/Smoke/Air---To use a phony rebate or trade value as the down payment instead of cash.

Mouse house---A finance company.

Double or triple mouse ---Multiple loans from different finance companies are needed to meet a large down payment on a car.

Over advance---A bank agrees to finance more than its standard lending policy would allow because the customer has a good credit rating.

Ace/Bullet/Gold/Brick/Rock--A customer with an excellent credit rating.

Baby--A first time buyer with little or no credit rating.

Skip---A transient credit customer.

Edgy/Flaky/Dinky--Has slow paying credit. Dinks mean delinquencies.

Scores Well---A customer application is strong and stable; good long term job, time at address, buying his home, good income and low debts.

BK/Banko--Bankruptcy.

Co-Maker, Maker, Co-X---Any co-signer, including spouses.

Odo---The legal form which states how many miles are on the vehicle at the time of purchase and whether the odometer has been altered.

Paper---Financing.

Pop---To repossess a vehicle, "Pop the car."

ABOUT THE AUTHOR

Greg Meakin is a New Hampshire native who grew up in Montreal. When he returned to the U.S., he embarked on a ten-year, award-winning career in the retail automotive business in Seattle, Washington.

He started in the car-rental industry as a sales representative, and soon became a statewide general manager.

A family-owned Seattle car dealership then offered him the opportunity to be its finance and insurance manager, and he rose to become the firm's general sales manager.

Over a few short years, he helped bring the dealership's revenues to record-breaking levels and won several regional and national awards for his efforts in the process.

This book evolved from the inside-out, primarily the result of Mr. Meakin's experience within the new-car dealership system. Much of the time, he and his colleagues wondered why people never simply requested a cost-plus deal.

When it later became vogue among consumers to drive hard bargains, they then wondered why consumers still wound up paying more than they needed to.

The car buyers who used the most aggressive and combative car-buying methods of the time, they observed, seemed to be the ones who were unhappiest with their car deals, for any number of reasons.

Mr. Meakin investigated this on his own, and the result was the No-Enemies Buying Method.

He used the method extensively, purchasing cars for friends and relatives, all with equally positive and money-saving outcomes. As a result of this success, he decided then to leave the retail car business to concentrate full-time on his discovery.

Mr. Meakin today lives in Venice, Florida, with his wife Deborah and three children--twin boys Carson and Colton, and their elder brother Tanner.

He heads his own corporation, which includes a publishing company, and a car buying service for consumers.

He also educates consumers and dealers alike concerning the No-Enemies Buying Method in print, seminars and personal appearances.

Those with questions regarding Mr. Meakin's professional work, those with comments on the No-Enemies car buying book, or comments on their car buying experiences are encouraged to write him. His business address is 509-A N. Tamiami Trail, Venice, FL, 34292, and phone calls to his business are welcomed at 813-485-8500.